# Meant to Be

# Meant to Be

## The Lives and Loves of a Jersey Girl

Lauren Pizza

Skyhorse Publishing

Skyhorse Publishing books may be purchased in bulk at special discounts for sales promotion, corporate gifts, fund-raising, or educational purposes. Special editions can also be created to specifications. For details, contact the Special Sales Department, Skyhorse Publishing, 307 West 36th Street, 11th Floor, New York, NY 10018 or info@skyhorsepublishing.com.

Skyhorse® and Skyhorse Publishing® are registered trademarks of Skyhorse Publishing, Inc.®, a Delaware corporation.

www.skyhorsepublishing.com

10 9 8 7 6 5 4 3 2 1

Library of Congress Cataloging-in-Publication Data is available on file.

Cover design by Barbara Leff

ISBN: 978-1-62914-332-3
E-book ISBN: 978-1-62914-333-0

Printed in the United States of America

# Contents

# Acknowledgments

———

There were moments when I thought the stories now in this book would never be told. I couldn't find the language, then I couldn't find the courage. Eventually, I simply wrote with faith. But I could not have done it without the confidence that others were nearby. My thanks to:

**Martin Levin**—so full of integrity and grace that you have no peer, and I'll never be able to repay your friendship

**Pat**—who read what I'd not yet written, saw what I'd not yet seen, and reminded me to laugh

**Alison**—thank you for my cover

**Laura**—you are an amazing friend for just listening and supporting this journey.

**Mallory**—you are truly a dedicated niece. I loved sharing time with you.

**My dear friends**, some of whom are related to me—you've shared my ups and tolerated my downs, and won my heart

**My editors Dana, Jennifer, Nicole, and Willa**—for your creative genius and, especially when I was unsure, your inspiration

**My Mom and Dad**—for sharing family stories and, even if you swallowed hard when you agreed, letting me tell them in public with humor

**My brother and sisters**—for loving me when I wasn't always so lovable, and for knowing how certainly I love you

**Joey and Jeffrey**—you are such an important part of my life and story

**Ariela and Danny**—gifts from God, on loan to me for this little while, I did not know that you were why I was meant to be

**Joe**—who came into my life and made all my dreams come true, even those I hardly dare to dream.

# Prologue

―

*Why do I want to write this book?*

Sam, my roommate from college, is just sitting there, blinking at me, expecting an answer to her question like it's the easiest thing in the world to articulate. But for once, I don't know what to say. I know what my husband, Joe, would say: it's "that time" in my life to do something creative. Christ, he makes it sound like menopause! I'm forty-friggin'-three! But it isn't really his fault. It's not like I told him the truth about why I'm doing this.

I could say it's because I want to reach other mothers out there—ones like me who used to hold down full-time, high-pressure jobs that they left to raise their children and now they chat about the Good Old Days, when they thought about things other than the sweater sale at Barney's or whether the neighbor really is having an affair with her landscaper (because in Palm Beach, we can read the *Shiny Sheet* to find out all the dirt; in New Jersey, we have to rely on word of mouth). For me, and for so many moms, raising kids is a constant challenge, and so much of it is about dealing with the guilt of not doing everything perfectly all the time—well, I'll be the first to admit that I fall on my ass on a regular basis, and it helps if we can all laugh about it together as we storm the next hill, whether it's a PTA meeting or an orthodontist appointment. Face it, laughing over coffee with your fellow moms is much more fun than crying with your therapist.

Or I could say I'm writing the book for me. It would also be nice to actually pursue a personal goal again, if only to stop my brain from turning to cottage cheese. Did you know the brain is a muscle? Well, it is, and like a glute or tricep, it turns to gelatinous muck if you don't use it.

Then again, I could always blame it on the kids. I want to write this book so I can get the hell out of my house and not be there when my eleven-year-old son comes home from camp and announces that he knows what sex is (courtesy of an older kid on the bus) or that he and his friends are planning an excursion into the "wilderness" (in other words, a local park) after which they'll hitch a ride home (from some serial killer, no doubt). Or when my thirteen-year-old daughter (who usually acts like she's *my* mother, telling me what to do and, more importantly, what *not* to wear—which, apparently, is anything in my closet or any piece of clothing not made of burlap; seriously, I think the girl was a Puritan in a former life) lies to my face about getting A's in school after I just read in her diary (that the little genius left open on her bed) about how she failed two tests and all she can think about is kissing this dirtbag boy from down the shore who doesn't seem to have parents. And that isn't even what bothers me the most! The worst part is the girl can't spell. I mean *redy* instead of *ready* and *wen* without the H? Is this what I'm paying to send them to private school for? But that's another story.

Why am I writing this book? You *really* want to know?

Why am I exposing all these parts of my life like a flasher to any stranger on the subway and lifting up the curtain on what people think is my glamorous lifestyle—traveling the world, meeting celebrities, and living in the same town as the Real Housewives of New Jersey? Why am I doing it?

"Because of my psychic," I finally say.

"Your *psychic*?" Sam is no longer blinking at me. She is now staring, with her mouth wide open.

Not long before I started this book, my best friend, Michelle, dragged me to a psychic. Don't get me wrong: I have believed in psychics ever since this guy—Jerry, a plumber from the Jersey shore—first read my palm. That was before I went away to college and before Jerry the Plumber went away to the insane asylum—at least that was the rumor—and it was definitely before I learned to stop letting strangers down the shore come up to me and touch my palm. But even before that—for most of my life, in fact—I knew I had heightened intuition and some psychic abilities of my own. Until now, I never shared that information with many people. Not since my mother took me gently aside and, in her usual, nurturing manner, explained, "What are you, crazy? Don't tell anyone that! They'll put you away!" If only someone had given Jerry the Plumber the same advice!

I don't believe in psychics the same way Michelle believes in psychics. She's like a cult member who not only drank the Kool-Aid, but snorted it in powder form. She'll spread her palm open for just about anyone who asks. Before she does, though, she strips off all her jewelry—including her wedding ring. Hell, half the people having affairs don't put in that much effort.

Michelle doesn't want to give the psychic any hints about her life, like that she's got a husband. She also doesn't want her husband to know she has a psychic. On her fortieth birthday she'd accidentally pocket-dialed her husband during a reading, and he was on the phone the whole time, including when she asked the psychic, "Did I marry the right guy? I mean, do you think I made the right decision?" So you can see why he's not so crazy about her visits. She always ends up getting caught anyway, no matter the situation. It was the same when she was a freshman in college and used her older roommate's ID. Michelle is a slim brunette. Her roommate was a heavy blonde. Even the blindest and kindest bouncers couldn't overlook that.

That's where I came in. Michelle heard about a psychic a few towns away and asked me to go with her as a cover-up so her husband didn't get suspicious.

Being a good friend, I agreed to go with her. We go way back. One of my first memories is holding Michelle's hand while we were in baby buggies together. Things obviously haven't changed much since then. As we drove to the appointment, she ducked down in her seat and made me do the same so nobody we knew could see us and report back to her husband. Then she parked miles away from the psychic's building so no one would spot her car in the lot. She also decided to lock her cell phone in the glove compartment.

Anyway, during the forty-minute hike from the car to the building, I could tell Michelle was getting nervous about lying to her husband. She asked, "Where do I tell him I was this afternoon?"

I looked around for a landmark. "You see that curtain store? Stop. Look at it carefully. Now close your eyes and visualize it. When he asks, picture it in your head and tell him you were with me shopping for curtains."

"What kind of curtains?" she asked.

"I don't know! How many kinds of curtains are there? Anyway, trust me—once you say the word *curtains*, men stop listening. It's like hypnosis. You can tell him you slept with his brother after that and he won't hear you."

"Do you really think I should?"

"Should what? Sleep with his brother? I don't know . . . Why don't you ask the psychic? Just make sure your phone is off."

"Very funny," she said. "No, I mean do you really think I should get new curtains?"

By then, Michelle's anxiety was rubbing off on me, and I wasn't in the mood for a reading with some psychic I'd never heard of. I could only imagine the kind of negative thoughts this woman would pick up on. Like something about me strangling my best friend with a curtain sash.

Luckily, when we got to the front door it was locked.

Michelle wasn't going to give up that easily.

"You have to call and find out where they are," she said. "I didn't go through all this sneaking around for nothing."

All this sneaking around? Like we'd just broken into the Pentagon! Christ, we drove a couple of miles and then walked twice that distance from the car. It wasn't exactly *The Bourne Identity*.

I had no choice but to call, since Michelle's phone was in lockdown in her glove compartment. I dialed the number and was told they were open, but the daughter would be coming down to do the reading instead of her mother.

For some reason this whole thing started to feel off; the energy was all wrong. As I walked up the steps, I decided not to get a reading done. Something about the setup made me feel like they were just doing it for the money, and to me, there's a little bit of evil in that. So I just sat there in the lobby, holding on to Michelle's wedding ring like a pawnbroker in Vegas, while the psychic's daughter told her what turned out to be a load of crap. Then I made up my mind to have a reading the next day with Pat, a nurse I knew with real psychic abilities. I trusted her. She had positive energy. Not to mention nice curtains.

"It was during that appointment that Pat told me I'd be writing this book," I explain to Sam, who seems to have forgotten what the original question was.

"Wait. Let me get this straight," she says. "You're writing a book about your life because your psychic told you to?"

She says it like I must be crazy.

"No. Not just because of the psychic. I think my great-grandmother had something to do with it too," I admitted.

"Your great-grandmother told you to write a book?" she repeated. At this point, I can't tell whether Sam is smirking or stifling a yawn.

"No, I never met my great-grandmother. She died before I was born. But I think I came back as her—you know, reincarnated. She always believed in psychics and all that. I think she's the reason I'm more open to the spiritual side of things, and I think that's the thread that goes through my life story."

So, okay, I wanted to write a book to do all those things—share my experience with other moms, hide from my kids, use my brain . . . and to talk about my experiences with the spiritual side of life.

"You're going to begin this book with your birth, when you came back as your great-grandmother?" Sam asked.

"Of course not," I responded. "People will think I'm crazy if I say that." My mother would be relieved. Sam obviously is too. That lasts for all of one second until I tell her, "I think I am going to start with when I died."

# 1

# The Lesson

———

I died when I was thirteen years old.

Thirteen-year-old girls are constantly dying of something: "Mom, if you dance like that in front of my friends, I will die of embarrassment." "Mom, I swear, if you don't stop stealing my bras and wearing them, I will die . . . besides, they're waaay too big for you." "Oh my God, Mom, I will absolutely crawl into the ground and die if you put that in the book!" (Okay, so maybe that's just my daughter.) But I did actually die at thirteen, as in I stopped breathing and had to be resuscitated. That's a hell of a lot worse than having to watch your mother dance at a house party while wearing your bra and then writing about it in a book, though my daughter may disagree.

This is what happened: My parents signed me up for summer sailing lessons down the shore at a place called Normandy Beach—because all the best sailing spots are named after World War II invasion points where we suffered massive casualties, right? I remember it being a pretty stormy day; the waves were rough, and we shouldn't have been out there in the first place. But, hey, I was the last of five kids, so my parents didn't seem overly concerned about a little thunderstorm heading my way.

Normally I would've been partnered up with Michelle, but the instructors had split us up, probably figuring we'd find a way to capsize the small Sunfish. Little did they realize that I could accomplish that just fine without her.

I was teamed up with an Indian girl I'd never met before. I remember she looked a little leery about being in a boat with me, and I have to admit I was a bit pissed off about that. In fact, that sort of doubtful expression on her face was the last thing I remember before our boat turned over and we were both dumped in the water.

I wasn't really panicked. More like annoyed. I mean, what the hell was I learning to sail for anyway? It wasn't like my parents owned a yacht. We were lower-middle class. We were lucky to own our station wagon!

Anyway, I kept my wits about me and decided just to swim and swim until I broke through the water. Smart, right? Except for one thing: I headed in the wrong direction, and instead of reaching the surface, I smacked into the sandy bottom. That narrowed my choices considerably.

I turned around and started swimming in the opposite direction. But at that point, I had already been under water for a few minutes and was running out of breath—fast. I headed in the direction of what I hoped was up. Then, I felt the bottom of the boat, felt the water enter my mouth, felt the blackness closing in around me . . . I remember thinking, "Oh, shit. I'm under the boat," and feeling very, very tired.

Then, I saw a light.

This is where everyone in my family says the same thing: "You didn't see a light! Don't be crazy, Lauren! Maybe you saw the sun." But there was no sun; we were in the middle of a storm! And, besides, what part of I was stuck under a boat don't they understand?

I went toward that light and was suddenly immersed in this feeling of love, peace, and happiness. It was like . . . well, it was like being slightly drunk at my eighth-grade dance. Only without getting sick from all those wine coolers.

I remember feeling bad for my family at the time, but, man, I was ready to go! If this was life after death, bring it on! Heaven was so much quieter than home, and I was filled with joy thinking that here I'd probably never need to wait for the bathroom.

Some people who have had post-death experiences say they were greeted by people they knew who had already passed on. But I was alone and completely at peace. None of my close family members had died yet, so there was no one to greet me; come to think of it, maybe that's why heaven was the calmest place I'd ever been.

Then I suddenly saw a face and thought, *God?* Followed by, God has a five o'clock shadow?

Nope. I was staring into the face of the man who rescued me. He and his friend had managed to pull me up on their boat and resuscitate me. Thanks. My soul was no longer up in heaven. It was down at the Jersey shore.

Had this happened to one of my kids, we probably would have had her airlifted to the nearest hospital, where she would have undergone about a million and one tests to make sure her lungs were fine and her brain was functioning properly. But back then, no one seemed that concerned. I eventually putted to shore on this little rowboat in the care of two complete strangers who let me off on the beach and then, just before heading off, thought to ask, "You sure you're okay?"

*Oh, yeah. You know, I wasn't doing so great there for a while. What with dying and all. But no problem now. It's cool.*

No one from the sailing school even bothered to check up on me, probably for fear of being sued. Nothing makes up for a little child endangerment like child neglect. I never saw that Indian girl again, but I hope she learned how to sail.

Once I was safely on dry land, I went to find my mother at her bridge game. When I told her what happened, she replied as only my mother could: "Well, you're fine now. You're fine! For God's sake, don't tell anyone you died. They'll think you're nuts! And I paid for those sailing lessons, so don't think for one second you're not going back out there tomorrow."

That was just marginally better than my father's response, which was: "God forbid you complain! Think of those nurses on the *Britannic*!"

To this day, I have no idea what that means.

I do know this: three good things came out of my drowning (four, if you count being resuscitated by a total stranger, who, as I recall, was kind of cute for an older guy). The first is that I realized, without a doubt, that death is not the end.

The next is that my death made me a local celebrity, though not at the time. My near-drowning wasn't in the papers or noticed by anyone, especially not my family. But just recently, I found myself surrounded by ten-year-old boys who all wanted to know what it was like to be a zombie. My son, apparently, told the story to his class, and they all leapt to the obvious conclusion: I had died, but I was still among the living, therefore, I must be undead.

But the best part of my death experience is that since then, I've been able to communicate with some of those who have passed on, which has brought comfort to others as well as to me. And I've had these dreams that aren't really dreams at all—more like predictions or psychic visions—that I've trusted to guide me through life.

When I was thirteen, I didn't know which way was up. But since then, I've known that I would always find my way.

I never did learn how to sail, though.

# 2

# Genes in a Blender

———

I have always known exactly where I'm from. I'm not saying that like it's something to be overly proud of. But your family history is something you can't change, though by all means you can lie your ass off about it. Most families enrich the lives of their members. My family has also enriched my therapist.

Each family starts by putting genes in a blender and seeing what comes out: always a mix of blessings and curses. In my case, the result is what you can call a good kind of crazy—if by "crazy" you don't mean exactly *crazy*. And if by "good" you don't mean exactly *good*. Well, let's just say my genes are mostly harmless—as in they haven't actually gone out and stabbed anyone yet. Except for that one time with my grandfather at my parents' wedding. This is what I heard about it from my mother: "It was three o'clock in the morning. A fight broke out at the reception. And Grandpa had his knife." Of course he did! Why wouldn't he? Some people only think to bring a gift and a nice card. I also know there was a bottle of whiskey involved (of course there was!), but I've never been able to get the whole story.

Apparently this wasn't the only wedding incident that has occurred in our family's history. My great-grandmother refused to come to the wedding of her only daughter (my grandmother) because she was marrying a Polish guy. Never mind that they all lived together in the same house—or that nobody really knows the difference between Hungarian and Polish anyway. Some families play board games together. My family starts fights at weddings. It's just something in our DNA. I think that particular gene may be getting watered down—there hasn't been a real fight at a wedding in our family in recent history, which is not to say there haven't been a few loudly whispered disagreements.

I have carefully and exhaustively conducted genealogical research into my ancestry (and by that I mean I asked my mom). I traced my family history three whole generations back, all the way to my great-grandmother, the one who I believe was reincarnated as me.

My great-grandmother, Elizabeth Farkas, came over to America from Hungary in 1896 at age eleven. She made the trip alone on a boat. Somehow she didn't capsize it.

Elizabeth was one of eleven girls, which made me hopeful that girls would run in my own family someday and made me sorry for my great-great-grandfather. To say he was outnumbered is an understatement; I just hope for his sake they didn't all get their periods at the same time.

When Elizabeth made it to Ellis Island, one of her older sisters, Marie, was there to greet her—but she never saw her other nine sisters or her parents again. Marie and Elizabeth were the only two to leave the "old country." Marie set her up to cook and clean for a Jewish family in Passaic, New Jersey. Elizabeth was only eleven, remember. She learned to speak English, but not to read it (which may explain our family's epic struggle with spelling), and she married my great-grandfather, Paul Fenstermach, who also had come from Hungary. When I asked about him, neither my aunt nor my mother had any idea how he and Elizabeth had met, but why should they? They only lived in the same house with them! This was before the Internet and iPhones, so her family didn't even have a good excuse to ignore each other.

Elizabeth's first daughter died at just a few weeks old. Her second daughter, an only child, was my Nana Elizabeth. Apparently, like George Foreman, my great-grandmother Elizabeth was not very original with names.

My great-grandmother was also five-foot-three and, again, like George Foreman, weighed about 250 pounds. She always wore a corset because Spanx had not been invented at the time. They owned a tenement building that my great-grandfather had inherited. It was my grandmother's job to bang on all the doors and collect the rent money. This was the Depression, and no one had any money for luxuries like food and rent. They eventually lost the building, and my great-grandfather was so distraught, he hung himself from the shower. Luckily, Elizabeth found him and, sturdy woman that she was, was able to cut him down. He settled for a slow death by alcohol and died from pancreatic cancer at age sixty-seven.

My great-grandmother was so tough that she went to the butcher's back room to cut the heads off her chickens herself. She would pluck the feathers to make pillows and blankets. Her homemaking skills must have skipped a generation or two because I am a complete failure in the kitchen. For some reason, maybe because they sense my great-grandmother in me, chickens seem to hate me, which only reinforces my notion that kitchens are not my natural habitat.

Elizabeth refused to use the automatic washing machine. She would wash clothes by hand until, after years of nagging from my aunt and mother, she finally gave in: she washed the clothes by hand first *and then* put them in the washing machine. That explains where I get my stubbornness.

Elizabeth was also very superstitious. You could not walk under a ladder. You could not have a baby shower until after the baby was born. You could not put shoes on the table (which seems to me more like an issue of hygiene than a superstition, but whatever). If you ate the crusts off bread, it would make your hair curly. Wish I'd known that before my unfortunate incident in eighth grade when I burned my forehead with a curling iron on the day of the class picture. Not a good look for me, and if I could have done the same thing by eating my bread crusts, I totally would have.

She also believed in witches and went to gypsies and fortunetellers. So that explains . . . well, it's pretty obvious, isn't it? But the good news is I have someone to blame! And that, after all, is what family is for.

As I mentioned before, I never met my great-grandmother in life; however, I have met her in a dream. Actually, I *think* I went to heaven. . . . In any event, it was when my grandmother was deathly ill, bedridden, and fading in and out of consciousness. In my dream, I saw Great-Grandmother Elizabeth holding a baby girl. I also saw her older sister, a friend of my grandmother's, Vi, and a dog. The next day, when I called my mother to see how my grandmother was doing, I told her about the dream. "Who is this woman Vi?" I asked. "She had a huge nose and wouldn't shut the hell up. I was trying to talk to the others, and she just wouldn't shut up . . ."

My mother told me that my grandmother had a close friend named Vi who had died many years earlier. She confirmed Vi had a big nose and bigger mouth. My grandparents had given the dog away because someone was allergic to it. I was glad to hear the pooch had rejoined my great-grandmother in the afterlife.

This all brings me back to my grandfather Milton (on my father's side), the one who started a knife fight at the wedding. He once ran against Jimmy Hoffa. If you ask me whether he had anything to do with Mr. Hoffa's disappearance, I might say yes, but afterward, I'd deny ever saying anything.

Milton was a huge flirt and an even huger presence. And by that I don't mean he had to wear a corset. He was the life of the party, and the ladies loved him. Milton would drive his station-wagon limousine to the Playboy Club, which he apparently had a stake in. And what self-respecting Playboy Bunny could resist a station-wagon limo? It was like Hugh Hefner meets Mike Brady.

I remember him wearing these enormous gaudy gold, turquoise, and silver rings in the shapes of Native American heads and horseshoes . . . which is not only a good look in itself, but is kind of like a fashionable version of brass knuckles. Probably no accident, since we are talking about the man who got in a knife fight at a wedding.

Anyway, what my Grandpa Milton made up for in charisma, he lacked in common sense when it came to raising kids (and, obviously, in picking out jewelry). When my dad was a child, Milton would take him to pool halls and bars. While other kids were in school, my dad was getting an education in life, which some people, including Milton, would say is infinitely more useful. If that had happened today, my father would have been snatched from the home faster than you can say "Child Protective Services." But back then, he was just spending quality time with his father.

Grandpa Milton moved his family from Newark to Springfield, New Jersey, where he had a modest home with two very large cement lions guarding the driveway. He had those same lions custom-made on one of his rings. It was all very *Sopranos* chic.

When we went to visit him, we were always greeted by a pit bull that seemed ready and able to eat us. Milton had a habit of skimming through the newspapers and finding these supposedly "family friendly" dogs listed right before the pound would put them to sleep. Some people might refer to them as "rescue dogs," but these were more like death-row inmates that had chewed up their previous owners like so many squeaky toys. I was terrified the entire time we were visiting my grandpa. The inside of his house looked like something you'd see on the TV show *Hoarders*. You had to go through a narrow pathway to get to the kitchen. The clutter was piled so high and deep, it was actually a good way to hide from the pit bulls.

Grandpa Milton also had this habit of never sitting in front of a window. When we met at Pal's Cabin in West Orange, he would always insist on sitting at the same table, facing the doorway. It was some serious Polish mafia-type stuff. He lived a long time, and when he finally died, he had about twenty storage units filled with more stuff. None of which contained Jimmy Hoffa's body, luckily for us.

Clearly my dad had quite the upbringing. He grew up in a small family: it was just him, Milton's brother's girlfriend's child, and, seventeen years later, a brother. You know, the typical American family, if by "typical" you mean the kind that you regularly see on *The Jerry Springer Show*.

My father always wanted a large family when he grew up—that is, until he actually had one. I remember him saying once that if he had it all to do again, he would choose death over having so many children. Nice. I mean, you can *think* it, like every other parent on the planet does, but do you really have to go and say it out loud? In front of all your kids? And on Father's Day? (I'm kidding, of course. I think it was Christmas.) But that's how both my parents were. They were never big believers in holding anything back.

When I was ten, my mother bought a florist's shop. She would drop me off at school, go to work, and then totally forget about me. I can understand running a little late every once in a while, but she would totally forget my entire existence, like I was just another flower delivery she dropped off and didn't have to come back for. I swear she would sometimes stand there, hand out, expecting my teacher to give her a tip for bringing me. After school, I'd watch as all the other kids' parents came to pick them up one by one, until it was just me and the teacher, who would have to call my mom to remind her—oh, I don't know—that *she had a daughter!*

I think this is why I have this anxiety about being on time. I mean, I get absolutely crazy if somebody's late.

My mother always says, "And I suppose you blame me for that? Well, what did you expect? You're the youngest of five! Of course I forgot about you sometimes. But you were fine. You were just fine. And you weren't alone—the teacher was there." Right. Because what could ever go wrong in that situation, well before anyone thought to do background checks on teachers? "Besides, I didn't want five kids. Your father made me have you." Oh, sorry, Mom, and thanks for sharing. Like it was *my* fault my parents had watched too many episodes of *Father Knows Best.*

By the time I was born, they'd already given up. They must have been having a grand old time, smoking and drinking the whole nine months I was in there. My sisters are all five-foot-nine. I'm five-one with small feet and hands. It's like, "Thanks, Mom and Dad. Thank you for the near-dwarfism."

When the members of my family took a chance and put their genes in a blender, some good things came out of it, too. They passed on to me their work ethic, their sense of loyalty, their craziness, and their survival skills.

But there was another vital ingredient in that blender. I saw the love between my parents—between all the screaming, that is. That ability to love deeply and genuinely has been passed on to me. Along with a taste for gaudy jewelry, a wariness about attending family weddings, and my great-grandmother's ability to connect with the spirit world.

# 3

# The Great Escape

———

Given all you've read so far, it may not come as much of a shock when I tell you that, as a child, I was always looking for ways to escape my four older siblings. Like any child blessed with natural creativity and a limitless imagination, I had two main forms of escape: TV and taking naps. Since I grew up in the seventies, there were lots of heartthrobs on television to fantasize about. There was Greg from *The Brady Bunch* (or even Mr. Brady, for little girls with daddy issues), there was David Cassidy from *The Partridge Family*, and, for the more adventurous among us, the two guys from *ChiPs*. But for me, there was really only one: Gopher from *The Love Boat*. You know what they say: "Aim high." No, wait . . . I mean: "There's something about a sailor."

When life in lower-middle-class New Jersey became too much, my brain would take me to *Happy Days* or *Fantasy Island*. My favorite daydream was the one where I got to sail away with Gopher on his cruise ship. I'd even get up to kiss the TV screen whenever he came on. Kind of makes you wonder where the parental supervision was. I mean, kids aren't supposed to get too close to the TV; it's bad for their eyes. (Look what happened to that little girl in *Poltergeist*.) I would dream that Captain

Stubing was my father, or that I was Julie, the cruise director, smiling and waving at the passengers as they boarded the boat. In fact, that was what I really wanted to be when I grew up: a professional waver. I would sit there during each hour-long episode and wave at the TV screen, practicing my perma-smile. I think I was the first six-year-old in history to develop carpal tunnel syndrome. And lockjaw. At the same time.

I believed in my fantasy world so much that I would sometimes forget where I was. My dad would come home from work and I'd be like, "Who are you and what have you done to Captain Stubing?"

This brings me to my other form of escape: napping. I absolutely loved it. I still do. I'm jealous of narcoleptics. My mother, of course, is the complete opposite. Around the house, she was like an exposed nerve. She had five kids, so you can't really blame her, but I do kind of wish that Xanax had hit the market a few decades sooner.

My mom hated for anybody to relax. It would make her crazy to see one of us at rest. My poor father hasn't slept since before their honeymoon. I had to find a place to hide to get some peace. My family would find me, after looking for me half-heartedly for a few hours, sleeping in the closet or in a laundry basket. . . . I could sleep anywhere, even standing up.

There was one last form of escape from our house: everyone always ran away to our grandmother's. My brothers, sisters, and I would take turns at it. If you saw one of us missing, you knew we were at Nana's house. I got so good at it that I was like a mini professional hobo. I would pack up my doll in a suitcase and walk up the hill to where my grandmother lived. I'd ring the doorbell and she would answer, almost as if she was expecting me. Which she probably was, considering I ran away every other week. Unlike my house, Nana's place was very calm, and I could take a nap anytime I wanted to. In fact, it was encouraged. Sometimes she would even nod off during dinner.

Okay, so maybe Nana's place was a little *too* calm, bordering on downright dull. She'd put on the Barry Manilow, break out the hard candy, and make up a bed on an equally hard mattress. But all of us kids went there for a break from our everyday lives and because we craved the one-on-one attention. My sister was so desperate for it that she ran away to an actual nursing home, where, the story goes, she convinced the more senile patients that she was their granddaughter. She probably could have been a successful con artist on the Atlantic City boardwalk.

As for me, I think my sense of escapism and belief in fantasy actually opened my mind to the more spiritual realm and to possibilities that are beyond everyday life. I believe in psychics. I believe in life after death. I believe that we can communicate with spirits. Hell, if I believed that Phyllis Diller and Kareem Abdul Jabbar could find long-lasting love on a one-week cruise aboard *The Love Boat,* then I'm pretty much open to anything.

What I believe most of all—and what my life has shown me—is that being open to people, ideas, and experiences that are not what you might expect, that don't fall within the well-defined lines of "normal," can lead to great things.

# 4

# Sleazeside

———

When I was growing up, family vacations meant the Jersey shore in all its fist-pumping, guido'ed-out glory. It's the East Coast's answer to the South's Redneck Riviera, and the perfect place to take your kids each summer to prepare them for a future of juvenile delinquency and early pregnancy.

What made it even better was that Michelle's grandparents had a shore house just four doors down from my grandparents' house. Now I'm not saying her grandparents were off-the-boat Italian, but if you went to their house in the middle of August, it'd be a hundred degrees and the sauce would have been on for like two days straight, boiling until it was the same consistency as molten lava.

The rest of the year, both sets of grandparents lived right next door to each other up in Clifton. Our parents, aunts, and uncles all grew up there together. And then Michelle and I were born and became best friends. So we're talking multilayered, multigenerational dysfunction here. I guess everyone thought it would be a good idea just to pack up the whole damn mess and move it down the shore each summer.

Michelle's grandparents and mine both had beach houses located right beside the bay. My parents, ever-vigilant about my safety when it didn't matter, would make me put on a friggin' life jacket just to walk two minutes to see her. It smelled like sweat and old crabs and the bright orange was more likely to attract unwanted attention than protect me. The important thing was that I wouldn't trip on the sidewalk and accidentally drown.

Since the beach house was more or less like taking our house and moving it down the Turnpike, "vacations" were no less chaotic than our regular life. I would still try to escape my mother's frantic energy by sneaking off and taking naps whenever and wherever I could.

One day they couldn't find me, and all hell broke loose. My parents went running to Michelle's house and then searched the bay, scanning the horizon for any sign of bobbing orange. My father finally found me asleep on a small child's chair in the upstairs closet. I could hear my mother's panicked voice screaming, "My God, is she okay? Does she have her life jacket on?"

Of course, when water safety really counted, no one wore a life jacket. My father would often take us out crabbing on the little rowboat he owned. Its tiny motor seemed too heavy for the vessel itself, which I think might have been made out of plywood stuck together with waterproof glue. All of us kids would pile aboard, crowding up front to balance out the weight of the motor. One good wave over the bow and my mother would be feeding fewer mouths for dinner.

When my father finally graduated to a larger boat with a proper engine, we started dragging lawn chairs on board instead of using actual boat seats. It was like *Sanford and Son* on the high seas.

The first time I got stung by a bee, I was on the boat with my father. My arm swelled up and I said, "I just got bit by a bee."

He said, "So? It's not like you got bit by a shark."

"What if I'm allergic?" I asked.

"Well, then you'd better have the antidote, 'cause it's not like there's any hospitals out here."

My mother—smart woman that she was—always hated going out on the boat. She claimed it was because of motion sickness, but I don't think that was the only reason. She also hated boats because of the amount of money my father spent on them over the years. He never bought a new one, so he'd always wind up paying a ton of money to get them fixed. It was a brilliant business plan. With what he spent on repairing junk boats, he probably could've bought a twenty-foot yacht.

I think my father was secretly happy that my mother was prone to seasickness because going out on the ocean or the bay was his escape. I loved it, too, because down below, near the anchor, I could lie down and take a nap, rocked to sleep by the waves—or possibly knocked unconscious by the boat fumes. It was peaceful until I had to pee. Then my father would pick me up and hold me out of the boat, right above the motor. It was some choice: either I held it in until my bladder burst or risked getting a leg chopped off. I could imagine my dad's reaction: "So what? You lost a leg. It's not like you got bit by a shark."

My father would also let each of us kids have a turn driving the boat, and he'd teach us all about boaters' rules. All I remember is that you pass on the right . . . I think. I never did get that straight. But I do vividly remember the screams of the other boaters when one of us was at the wheel.

When we were down the shore, Michelle and I were inseparable. We went from being pushed in our strollers together to riding our first little tricycles together to going on bike rides together to eventually riding in the back of cop cars together. Our parents were so proud.

We both had our first jobs at Waterworks in Seaside, also affectionately known as "Sleazeside," where you could find more tattoos and mullets than anywhere else in the state. And I'm not talking about the fish.

Waterworks was an amusement park with a huge waterslide, and our job was to stand at the top of it and tell the people in line when it was their turn to slide down. So basically Michelle and I would be there all day—both in our bikinis, me with Sun-In in my hair (going from my natural blonde to albino white) and slathered in enough tanning oil to spit-roast a small pig—telling people, "Go . . . Go . . . Go. . . ."

Michelle would literally talk all day. If her jaw had been wired shut, she would have had to learn sign language. She could remember every name and every little detail of anyone we'd ever met in our entire lives. Guys I'd try to forget, she would remember their names, addresses, and inmate numbers. I was amazed by how her mind worked. We would spend the day talking about boys and clothes and absolutely nothing for eight hours a day: "Oh my God, Lauren, did you see that guy . . . Go

. . . who came over to me last night . . . Go. . . and gave me his phone number . . . Go. . . ." And we actually got *paid* to do this. Because, as you know, any job you can do in a bikini requires specialized skill sets and a high level of training.

Sometimes our boss would switch it up a little and have us work at the exit of the ride. People would come down this steep slide, and the thing was like a friggin' enema. Water would shoot up their asses, and their bathing suits would be permanently wedged between their butt cheeks. Michelle and I would be there at the bottom to point the way to the bathroom. Glamorous. I'm pretty sure that was how Julie from *The Love Boat* got her start.

I did have another amazing job before that: picking up garbage off the beach. It was perfect work for a kid. I got fifty cents an hour and all the broken bottles and used condoms I could carry.

Life down the shore was not only about work. When Michelle and I were finally old enough to get into the clubs—and by "old enough," I mean underage jailbait—we would leave our grandparents' houses in one outfit, carry clothes with us, and then find somewhere on the boardwalk to change. Our heels would be higher, our skirts would be higher, our hair would be higher, and we'd pack on the makeup by the pound. We'd start out looking like innocent schoolgirls and end up like prostitutes who'd joined the circus. Then we'd go into the club, and Michelle would tell every guy there she was a virgin. For as long as I've known her, she's always been a virgin, no matter how many guys she's been with. I'd tell her, "Michelle, it doesn't work that way. It's not like an octopus arm. It doesn't grow back!" But she didn't care.

These days, Michelle and I both have children about the same age, and we've continued the family tradition of spending our summers at the Jersey shore. The craziness has made it to yet another generation. Only now, instead of a life jacket, I'm thinking of making my daughter wear a chastity belt when she leaves the beach house. If I can find one in bright orange.

# 5

# Art the Driver

———

Remember, my mother bought a florist shop when I was ten. For a while, my summers at the shore were replaced with slave labor. At least I finally figured out why my parents had all those kids! They had their own little sweatshop going. We were like a factory in China, or one of those big farm families where the six-year-old is driving the tractor and the three-year-old is out strangling chickens for dinner so everyone can eat, only we were making floral arrangements for weddings and funerals.

Since Michelle and I were inseparable, it was only natural that she came and endured the forced labor with me. Working with Michelle, as much as I loved her, drove me crazy. I could finish an entire wedding arrangement by the time it took her to get off the phone with one single customer. She'd get their whole life story when all she needed was their address. Even my father would say, "Damn it, Michelle, do I have to light a fire under your ass? You're like a useless goddamn snail." And that's the way he spoke to *other people's* children.

But the truth is that hidden under all their layers of craziness, my parents are kind people who would take anybody in. They are like Brad and Angelina. Or any college I got accepted to. That's how Art the driver came into our lives.

Art was already retired when he started delivering for the previous florist, but he didn't want to go home and have to spend time with his wife, so he came to work for us. "Work," in this instance, meant that for five dollars an hour he would take me along on deliveries to haul heavy floral arrangements bigger than I was to the doors while he smoked in the truck. Between deliveries, he'd stop by the bowling alley, where he'd leave me in the parked van with the window rolled down, like a dog, while he sat at the bar getting a few beers. Then we'd drive to our next delivery, and he would swear nonstop like a sailor the whole time. In short, he was my hero.

Like my Grandpa Milton, Art loved women, with the possible exception of the one he'd married. He liked nothing better than delivering dozens of roses and seeing the smiles they brought to women's faces. But there were some customers who weren't so willing to accept our deliveries, especially when they came from cheating boyfriends or husbands who had forgotten anniversaries or as any other kind of peace offering for the messed-up shit men do. (Here's a hint to all you guys out there: when you're asking for forgiveness—which you no doubt will need to do at some point—never give a woman anything that requires snipping. It will only put ideas in her head.)

But Art knew very well that my mother's rule was, "Don't bring any flowers back. I don't care what you have to do with them." Art would try to convince the customers to accept the deliveries. "Look, the guy may be a jerk, but don't take it out on these beautiful roses," he'd say. Between his binge drinking at the bowling alley and his counseling sessions on the customers' front steps, it's a wonder we ever got anything delivered.

To me, Art was more like a grandfather than a coworker. Before retiring, he'd owned a gas station, and he always carried enough cash in his wallet to put a stripper through med school. At lunch time, he'd drive us to his favorite hot dog stand, which was this scary van near inner-city Paterson run by a blind guy. I was pretty sure some of those hot dogs were older than I was. Seriously, this was the kind of place where instead of coleslaw you would get a side of *E. coli*. The only reason it was still in operation was the health inspectors kept getting carjacked on the way there. Apparently Art loved the hot dogs so much he was willing to risk my life for them.

Art was always there for me. He was the one who picked me up from the hospital after I got my wisdom teeth out. My dad's insurance would only cover the procedure if it was done at a hospital, so that was where my mom dropped me off. After it was over, I was too doped up and swollen even to know where I was, but I knew Art's number and he came to get me.

I believe people come into your life for a reason. Art was the first of many people whom I met by chance, by luck, or by fate, who became an important part of my life and helped me when I needed someone to be there for me. I could have rejected him because he was strange or scary, but even as a ten-year-old, I could tell Art had a good heart. Sometimes people come into my life to help me, and sometimes I come into someone's life to help them. Either way, it's those connections that can change a life.

# 6

# ADD and Subtract

———

Between spending summers at the Jersey shore and breaking child labor laws at my family's florist shop, there was the small matter of school to deal with. I absolutely loved school. The social part of it anyway. It was just all that learning I couldn't really give a crap about.

Since kindergarten I'd always had crushes and "boyfriends" I'd pass notes to, saying how much I liked them (and probably begging them for rides home). I'd sit in class not paying attention to anything the teacher said, staring out into the hallway and waiting for some boy I liked to pass by. Today they might diagnose me with ADD. Back then it was a "visual perception problem." I'm pretty sure my ability to focus in class was mostly disrupted by raging hormones.

The funny thing is that I never even had a clue about what sex was until I was almost in high school. That's because my parents, who would blurt out the most inappropriate things (for example, my father said to me, "Your mother would've stopped at four kids, you know. *I'm* the one who wanted to have one more"), held back when it came to just one topic: any kind of talk about sex. I grew up thinking that you got pregnant from swallowing a pill. And my dad's big sex speech didn't exactly help matters much. He said, "Don't let yourself become locker-room talk." *Great, Dad, big help considering I'd never been in a boys' locker room!* I figured they talked about baseball and football and basketball, and for years after that I was too traumatized to play any organized sports, let alone handle any balls.

I did, however, manage to try out for cheerleading. Let's just say it didn't go so well. When it was my turn, I blanked out and forgot every single word to the cheer. I couldn't even remember the name of my school's football team! A Rhodes Scholar I was not.

To rescue any hopes they had of me living on my own someday, my parents sent me to preparatory school in ninth grade. Don't get the wrong idea. Neumann Prep wasn't exactly where the Kennedys sent their kids. It was one of the more affordably priced private schools in the area—Wayne, New Jersey, just a short bus ride through what looked like downtown Beirut.

When I got there, I landed right in the lower-level classes—the kind of courses that prep you less for college than for a career at Burger King. Everyone else in ninth grade was reading *The Crucible*. I was reading *The Outsiders*. My father showed an active interest in my education by saying, "I can't believe they put you in those classes and your mother didn't do anything about it." But that was after I graduated. From college.

It's not like I was sitting in the back of the class eating paste and counting to ten on my fingers. If I needed to focus and learn, I did. It's just that I had better things to think about than schoolwork—like my fantasy world. And sometimes even real life. By the time high school rolled around, I was spending less time studying math and more time studying the cute boys who roamed the mall in packs. And come 9:00 p.m. on a hot summer night, full of nervous energy after napping half the day away, I did anything and everything to get out of my house so I could meet up with my friends. I'd kill my kids if they tried it, but as I keep reminding them, it was a safer world back then.

Luckily not all my friends were like me. Some of them didn't have a life, fantasy or otherwise—like Marie, a girl I'd met on the bus to Neumann Prep. She was the one focused student in a school bus full of hormone-driven teenagers. She was also the girl who had to be school president, be on every committee, get straight A's, and just be a general pain in the ass by making me feel like I must have been dropped on my head at birth. After an exam, I'd walk out of class feeling like I'd just gotten my ass kicked by algebra. I'd say to Marie, "Oh my God, I failed that test." She'd say, "Oh my God, me, too. I failed it, too." The next day she'd get a ninety-eight. I'd get a twelve.

Somehow Marie could study all night and get by on a few hours of sleep. And this was before they'd invented Red Bull. Most of my other friends would have been happy to hibernate the whole four years, waking up on occasion to smoke, get laid, and reapply their hairspray before going back to sleep.

While I wasn't quite that bad, I would be on the phone with my boyfriend every night until three in the morning. Then I'd wake up four hours later unable to remember a single SAT word from the entire fifteen minutes I'd studied. By the time my kids reached third grade, I had to stop helping them with their math homework. I'd be like, "How should I know? Maybe we should call Marie and ask her."

Marie's parents were the exact opposite of mine. Not only had they never forgotten her at school like she was some kind of ward of the state, but they would actually check her homework and make sure she was doing well. I would look at Marie and think, *Damn, am I lucky! Who needs their parents getting involved in school?*

I'm not saying that my parents never got involved in my education. They did, and from what I remember, it was always a complete disaster. After school I used to go to private tutoring to get my grades up. My dad would come to pick me up and ask, "How was dope school today?" Then we'd spend the rest of the drive home listening to Howard Stern interviewing strippers. Not only was it educational, but it was also a great bonding experience.

I guess I was lucky because my dad had low expectations of me from the start—at least since kindergarten, when he'd seen me doing my homework and spelling "han" instead of "hen." He'd looked at me horrified, like he was thinking, *How could I have produced the stupidest kid on earth?* I looked at him like, *When in the hell am I ever going to need to spell "hen"?* And we both just seemed to decide there and then that academics and any job where livestock might be involved were not in the cards for me.

This point may have been driven home by the high school talent show. My parents finally dragged their asses to a school event and saw their daughter onstage with Marie and five of our friends, all wearing fluorescent outfits and looking like hookers. In case you're wondering what our talent was, we were Seven in Heaven, singing, bumping, and grinding our way through a song we'd written: "We're Seven in Heaven and We Like to Boom." Seriously, don't you have to try out for these shows? What teacher watched our audition and decided this would be wholesome entertainment for the entire student body and their families? But somehow there we were, up on stage, basically singing about how we liked to have sex. *Proud* is not quite how my parents were feeling. *Mortified* is more like it. But at least I remembered all the words.

Every single girl in that group went on to be a success: three lawyers, one doctor, one nurse, one human resources manager for Goldman Sachs, and me, the former manager of a computer tech consultancy firm and now a writer. What does that say to me? You don't always have to bust your ass in school to see your success boom.

# 7

# The Y Factor

———

What is it about Y chromosomes that turn seemingly normal people into
. . . well, guys? While Michelle, Marie, and I have always been as close as
sisters (I'd say "sistas," but I'm a few shades too pale to pull that off), and
I have three actual sisters of my own, there has always been a strong male
presence in my life. But I still consider them an alien species. I mean,
seriously, half the time I don't know what they're thinking, and the other
half I know they're not thinking at all.

I blame my brother for setting my expectations too high. He says he
never really gave being "the only boy" much thought—he just remem-
bers that my mom brought a new baby girl home every year and he just
figured life was like that. When I was a toddler and he was about eight,
my parents had the two of us share a bedroom. I'd wake up in the morning and look over the side of my crib to see if my brother was up. He
would be sleeping peacefully, but I thought I could wake him with my
steely, infant stare. After about a minute of that crap, I would think, *Let's
start the day*, and I'd throw my plastic elephant at him. Then I'd stand up
in my crib and wait for him to stir. Nothing. I would feel disappointed
because I had nothing else to throw at him, and he still was not moving.

Then all of a sudden his eyes would open and he'd throw the elephant back into my crib.

My brother would pull me up from my crib and walk hand in hand with me to the kitchen, where I would climb up on my high chair. He would get a bowl of cereal out for me, pour the milk, and hand me a spoon. When I got older, I moved into the bedroom with my sisters. That wasn't the end of the special treatment, though. My father worked three jobs and wasn't around much, so it was my brother who helped us with book reports and protected us from bullies . . . and all other boys, actually. None of his friends knew he had four sisters—he wouldn't let them anywhere near us.

Our street was filled with kids, and we roamed freely from one house to the next. I don't really remember any adults ever being there. It was like *Lord of the Flies* except without any wild pigs to kill. But the squirrels in the neighborhood were terrified, rarely having a moment of peace to gather their acorns without dozens of screaming kids running through the yards.

Looking back on it, our adventures in my backyard by the stream were every kid's dream. The boys on the block would be either cowboys or Indians, and the girls were either the cowgirls or the Indian squaws getting captured. Sure, it seems a little sexist now. But I actually liked being captured because I would have the full attention of a cowboy or an Indian, who would hold my hand and bring me over to a tree. To this day, I still have a thing for guys in cowboy hats. Or feathered headdresses. So, basically, half the Village People.

One of my closest friends throughout childhood was my cousin, Anthony. We'd have adventures that bordered on juvenile delinquency, but we always looked out for each other. Our criminal code of ethics was: be prepared to lie for each other, never rat the other one out, and he could hook up with my friends but I was off-limits to his. No, I wasn't just off-limits—I was a friggin' leper. Whenever we went to school dances, if a boy started talking to me and found out I was Anthony's cousin, he'd walk away faster than if I'd said, "Hey, I heard getting pregnant is a good way to get out of gym class."

But my cousin and I are really similar in a lot of ways. I sometimes think that if I were a boy, I would be Anthony. And if Anthony were a girl, he'd be Jersey's answer to Lolita. We went to Neumann Prep High

School together, where he always seemed to be surrounded by female admirers. I think in the yearbook he was named Most Likely to Take Over for Hugh Hefner.

Anthony has always been protective of me, ever since we were little kids. I remember playing on the slide one time and falling off it onto my head. The last thing I saw was Anthony running as fast as he could, like Lassie on two legs, to get an adult to help. Unfortunately the adult he got was my father. You know how they say not to move someone who may have a concussion? Well, my father obviously didn't. He picked me up, took me home, and called the pediatrician, who was willing to make a house call because he was just coming home from a wedding. Now, think about it. What do people do at weddings? They either get married or get drunk. And the doctor wasn't getting married. So he came to check me out, looked under my eyelids, felt my head, and declared I was fine. Right after that, I passed out. Not from a concussion but from the smell of alcohol on his breath.

After that I gave up falling off slides and started falling for boys—though in both cases I seemed to land on my head. Anthony was there for me then, too. He rode shotgun with me when I just *had* to deliver a note to some boy who had broken up with me. I'd written a long letter to this guy telling him how he'd hurt me—because you know how effective that is. I cried my eyes out while writing. The letter was tear-stained, mascara-stained, snot-stained. I gave it to this boy who broke my heart. He probably read maybe the first two sentences of my ten-page manifesto about what an asshole he was for dumping me, then threw the damn thing out, glad he dodged that bullet. It's different now—girls today have texting and can embarrass themselves much more quickly, but at least without the snot.

Anyway, Anthony and I pulled up to this guy's house, and I jumped out to put the letter in his mailbox. Then I ran back to the car and took off like a bat out of hell, sideswiping a parked car in the process, which I hoped belonged to whatever new girl he was seeing. I didn't stick around to find out.

When I got home, I parked the car and left it. My father didn't notice the damage until the next day. Then I heard him screaming, "Lauren, what did you do to the goddamn car?" Like it was a Ferrari instead of a Ford.

I played dumb—and apparently I was so good at it that my father actually believed I didn't do it and I was just covering for one of my friends. To this day, at family get-togethers, when Anthony and I reminisce, he'll say, "Hey, remember that time you hit that . . . ow." That's as far as he goes before I bury my heel in his shin. It's the one time in my life I actually got away with something, and I don't need my cousin confessing to my parents now.

My brother and my cousin both made sure that, when it came to guys, I had high standards—or at least, I would *eventually* have high standards. I was lucky to have them, as well as my dad, as role models for how men are supposed to treat women.

# 8

# Touched by an Angel

———

I have always been surrounded by angels. I'm not talking about my cousin Anthony or my brother, either. It was clear early on that I needed the angels on my side—not only to protect me from the boys in the neighborhood (what with those cowboys-and-Indians slightly *Shades of Grey*ish episodes that took place in my back yard), but to protect me from myself.

After my drowning experience at age thirteen, I had a few other near-death episodes that involved Anthony, Marie, and an ice-covered road. (To get a flavor for the incident, I recommend waiting for the next winter storm, taking your cousin's piece of crap Fiat out for a drive, rounding a corner at top speed, and seeing what happens. Please send your written testimonial or notice of a class-action lawsuit directly to my publishers.)

The three of us were also in a car together when we hydroplaned and were literally lifted off the road. We came down and skidded to a stop in front of a funeral parlor. The symbolism was almost too much to take.

I truly believe I survived these situations because my angels were always looking out for me.

Yes, angels, plural. I may curse, I may occasionally get drunk and take my top off at the beach, and I may have committed some other minor crimes and misdemeanors, but that doesn't mean angels don't follow me around. In fact, I think the angels are loving it! They don't see much action up there, and I'm pretty sure God blocks all episodes of *The Jersey Shore*.

I do have proof of communicating with angels, or at least with spirits that have passed to the other side. And by "proof," I mean it's written down in black and white (right here), so it must be true.

After my death experience from the drowning incident, I developed heightened intuition and dreams that seemed to reflect psychic abilities or the capacity to communicate with those who have died. Believe me, I didn't sign up for it. It's not like I paid extra to have it as part of my phone plan. It was just sort of something that happened.

One of the first times I experienced this was with my first boyfriend's brother, Tommy. When I was fourteen or fifteen years old, I met Nick at our private school, and we started dating. Unlike my family—who sent me there because there were no convenient nunneries in the area—Nick's parents were wealthy and actually wanted to invest in his education and future. So you can imagine how thrilled they were when he brought me home.

I have always fallen hard for the guys I've dated, and Nick was the first of that long line. (Well, not counting Gopher from *The Love Boat*, whom I always remained faithful to . . . at least until *Happy Days* came on.) We had this amazingly sweet relationship, and it didn't hurt that his dad had a driver and would send us to the city in his private limo. That was my first introduction to real money. It was fun. It wasn't why I loved Nick, though it did put a sort of romance-movie spin on our teenage dating. I remember telling Nick, "If we're not together in ten years' time, let's promise to meet here on New Year's Eve."

As a teenager, I didn't have a great sense of romance. I said this to him, not on the top of the Empire State Building or on the Brooklyn Bridge, but instead at South Street Seaport. I vaguely remember the smells of dead fish and stale urine. But the point is, I'm a strong believer in everlasting love. And air fresheners.

Once Nick told me the story about his brother's death, I knew the love between them hadn't died, and I started talking to Tommy regularly. We'd never met in real life, but we had a connection. I felt like there was a higher power bringing us together. Plus I was receptive—open to the more spiritual side of life—and Tommy was communicative, unlike most guys who were still alive.

The first time I contacted Tommy was when I wanted to get in touch with his brother. Okay, not the most spiritual use of this gift. But this was before texting, so my options were limited. I hadn't spoken to Nick for several days, and I finally said, "Oh, Tommy, please let your brother call me." Not long after, the phone rang. It was Nick. I remember thinking, *Wow, it worked.*

Later in life, when my confidence in my intuition and abilities grew, my Nana, who had died, came to me in a dream. My father's health wasn't good, she said, and he was in for a tough ride. But she wanted to assure me that he would be all right in the end.

I immediately called to tell my mother, thinking it would bring her comfort. Her response? "Jesus Christ, why the hell do you talk like that? You sound like a nut! If you call your father and tell him that, you'll only stress him out. Do not call him. Okay?"

So I said, "Okay." Then I hung up the phone and immediately called my father.

"Dad, Nana said you're going to be all right, but you need to take better care of your health in order to recuperate."

His mother's words really seemed to reassure him, and he honestly felt that the message was coming from her. "Lauren must have spoken to my mother," he reasoned. "How the hell else would she know the word 'recuperate'?" *Thanks, Dad. Your faith in me is so sweet.*

Within twenty-four hours of my grandmother's visit, my father was rushed into emergency surgery; his gall bladder had literally exploded. He could have died on the operating table—no doubt the "tough ride" my Nana was talking about—but just as she'd told me, everything turned out okay. And as the rest of my family and I stood over his hospital bed nearly crying with relief, I had the added bonus of giving my mother a "told ya Nana was talking to me" look.

This was just one of the times that I heard from the other side. I know it sounds crazy if you haven't experienced it, and you may put it down to wishful dreaming, coincidence, or something, but, hey—it's my book.

# 9

# Give Me Your Hand

—

Remember Jerry the Plumber—sorry . . . Jerry the *Psychic* Plumber? The one Michelle and I met down the shore? He had an impact on my life, though he may not exactly qualify as an angel in the usual sense. For one thing, angels don't normally fix sinks with their ass cracks hanging out. At least, that's not what *my* picture of heaven looks like.

But Jerry did have a gift that he shared with me—and I don't mean his ability to talk to pretty girls at the beach. Our first conversation went something like this:

Jerry: "Hey. Do you ladies mind if I take a look at your palms? I can read your future."

Me: "Uhhh . . . sure, stranger."

Being an utter genius and a recent high school graduate, I proceeded to hold out my hand and let this unknown man with a mullet trace the lines on my palm with his finger. For all I knew, this was his way of picking up girls. Turned out this guy was the real deal. He had genuine psychic powers, and he never asked for a thing in return.

Jerry was my first—psychic, that is—and I have to admit I was a little bit skeptical of his reading in the beginning, especially when he told me, "You'll be going to college soon. I see a girl with many C's."

*No shit!* I figured that was me, maintaining an awesome 2.0 grade point average and making my family proud. But then he went on to tell me that this girl and I would have nothing in common and we wouldn't get along at all. Okay, that I could accept. It wasn't like I wore matching monogrammed sweaters with my classmates at prep school, so it was possible I'd be a bit of an outsider at college as well.

The next thing he told me was that I would get mixed up with a meathead at school who would be into partying hard. Well, that one just seemed a little obvious. Hello? There I was with Michelle at the Jersey shore, my hair higher than Marge Simpson's. It wasn't like we were there to meet Nobel laureates. Meatheads were pretty much my type. But he also said I'd come through the relationship and the breakup fine, so I didn't worry much about it. I just hoped Mr. Meathead would be fun while he lasted—more sirloin than weenie.

Jerry also said that my grandfather would pass away while I was in college. While this didn't exactly make his predictions come across as a fun party trick, it also didn't seem all that shocking, considering my grandfather's age and health.

But his next prediction was the one I didn't see coming: "Your first husband will die before you do, but you won't be unhappy about it."

"What? What do you mean I won't be unhappy? I don't kill him, do I? Do I freakin' kill him?"

At that point, Jerry actually took a step back, as if I were possibly going to kill him, too. "No, I'm just saying it will be okay. You'll be all right with it. Also, you'll never need to worry about money again, and you'll be known for your creativity."

Hmmm . . . okay. That seemed a little unlikely. Unless I won first place in a flower-arranging contest and they judged on speed rather than aesthetics, and the prize just happened to be, oh, a billion dollars, I couldn't imagine how money wasn't going to be an issue or how I'd get famous for my floral creations. Jerry was a plumber, after all—so maybe he specialized in pipe dreams. But he seemed pretty sure of himself, and that put me at ease.

I tucked those predictions away in the back of my mind, in that space behind all the Guns N' Roses lyrics where algebra used to be, and concentrated on my future. And by that I mean I went to work on my tan.

# 10

# Everything I Never Needed to Know I Forgot from College

Here's the thing with college. You know how they tell you to apply to two dream schools, two probable schools, and two safety schools? For me, the safety schools *were* my dream schools, because it was my dream that even they would accept me. Okay, so I'm not saying it was a great dream, not like Martin Luther King, Jr. or something: "I have a dream that someday I will get accepted to a college that doesn't have the word 'community' in its name."

The bad news was that my SAT scores were less than stellar—I don't think I even broke a thousand, which placed me somewhere between the SPED kids and a fulfilling career as a waitress—and my options were limited. The good news was that I saved my parents a shitload of money on applications because I only sent out three. You're welcome, Mom and Dad.

At the college prep school my parents sent me to (or, as they would say, "worked like slaves to send me to," although, despite the fact that I didn't do great in history, I'm pretty sure slaves did not save up nice nest eggs to send their kids to private high schools), the selling point was that 99 percent of students went on to college. My parents always had confidence in me; in fact, they were confident I'd be in the 1 percent that didn't go. My three sisters had to show off and all attend Villanova. But I was freaking thrilled to get accepted to the University of Dayton in Ohio, which I like to think of as the Villanova of the Midwest (though I might have confused it with Daytona, Florida, when I sent out the actual application; I didn't do great in geography either).

The point is that I picked the University of Dayton to get away from the family business. Or, more precisely, to get away from the family *and* the business. Finally I would be free from the florist shop.

I'll never forget my interview at the university. My father went with me on the ten-hour drive to Ohio, and he was so desperate to have them accept me that he bartered my services: "Please take her. She'll plant the flowers on campus. She's good at that. She'll do anything. You've gotta take her." He would've been great in an arranged wedding, marrying me off for a diseased donkey and maybe a chicken or two. "Seriously, forget the chickens. Tell you what: give me an Egg McMuffin and let's call it even. Just take her off my hands."

But the truth is that my dad was actually really helpful on this one occasion—if we stretch the definition of "helpful" to include very embarrassing, a little inept, and quite possibly as traumatized as I was by the whole experience. His idea of researching the campus was to drive through the ghetto where the students lived and ask some kid at random, "Hey, what do you think about the school?"

This guy said, "Come on in . . . Let me tell you about it." We proceeded to follow him into his apartment, where he took us to sit in the dining room. There was stuff all over the table, so he said, "Hold on. Let me clear that for you," and in one sweep of his arm knocked everything onto the floor—I mean dirty dishes, pizza boxes, books, and what looked suspiciously like a bottle of roofies. Then he said, "Sit down," and we did.

Something about this situation must have instilled my father with a great sense of confidence, because he allowed his youngest daughter to attend the school. That whole student ghetto was like one giant frat house, a free clinic, or possibly a holding pen. Either way, I guess, Dad thought it was good enough for me.

As for my decision, when I heard that the school's ratio of women to men was one to eight, I decided right there and then I was going to go. I also decided against getting busy on anyone's dining room table. In that case, protection wouldn't be just a condom; it would mean a full hazmat suit and a can of roach spray.

I'll never forget the day I moved away to college. I came home straight from clubbing in Seaside, packed up my 1980 Malibu (just my luck—the letters on my license plate spelled "COW," which is a really attractive message you want to be flashing to other drivers), and made the trip alone. My dad had gotten that car from a closing for five hundred dollars. It was a barter, and there was no bill of ownership. Another great feature was that the gas tank was hidden under the license plate. Whenever my friends borrowed my car, they would always say, "I wanted to fill the tank up for you but I couldn't find it." So they'd just give me the five dollars instead.

It took me about eleven hours to drive to Dayton, and this was at a time when there were no cell phones. I'd pull over at a truck stop, lock all the doors, and fall asleep for a while, secure in the notion that no one could easily pop open the locks on my old clunker with a wire hanger, and that it was perfectly safe to let your guard down at truck stops.

I might not have known much about geography before I started school at Dayton. But by the time I made it there, I knew this: holy crap, Pennsylvania is a huge state. Already I was learning.

When I got to my dorm, I met my roommate—a girl from Columbus with the initials C. C. Turned out Jerry the Plumber was right: C. C. and I couldn't have had less in common. I was straight from the shore; she was straight off the farm.

All I remember is that I cried that first day because I felt like I didn't belong. Then I thought of home and realized that being stuck out on a farm in the middle of the Corn Belt wasn't so bad after all. Hell, the worst that could happen was that the children of the corn would emerge and drag me off to satisfy He Who Walks Behind the Rows. Still better than sitting through one of my mother's lectures.

For the first few weeks of school, I wasn't happy. I actually missed New Jersey. I think I was going through physical withdrawal from the fumes on the Jersey Turnpike. I'd catch myself inhaling really hard at gas stations in Dayton: "Yeah, that's it. . . . Now just add a little tanning oil and hairspray and we're good to go."

My sister suggested I have a party in my dorm room and invite as many people as possible. I did exactly what she said: I went out, got a big bowl of beer, threw a party, and was written up that night and put on probation for violating college code. *Thanks, sis, big help.* That really made me love school a whole lot more.

Things quickly got better when I met Nancy, another girl from New Jersey. I think we recognized each other by how high our hair was. In those days, I was always walking around in a fog of industrial-strength Volumaxx. If that stuff can eat through the ozone layer, imagine what it does to brain cells.

Nancy and I were actually pretty smart—well, smarter than her father, anyway, who had given her a gas station credit card. Little did he know there was an off-campus gas station with a liquor store attached to it—because what better way to send the "don't drink and drive" message to a bunch of college students? Nancy and I would charge about eight hundred dollars a month there, "filling up" on everything from wine coolers to whiskey. The only thing we never seemed to get was gas. And it's a good thing, because we probably would have drunk that, too.

I met another lifelong friend, Sam, at Dayton, too. It didn't seem that way at the start, though. I walked into a dorm meeting and there she was, dressed in what looked like a Laura Ashley nightgown. I was standing there in my best high-class hooker look thinking, *Who the hell wears that?* It was like something you'd dress a Victorian doll in. Another one straight off the farm.

Sam, though, as it turned out, was not a prude like C. C. She was more like a Playboy Bunny dressed in farmer's clothing—and I mean that in a good way. Under that Mama Cass muumuu tent she wore was hidden a perfect pair of double D's. If I'd owned those babies, I'd have been running around in a bikini top all day, flashing strangers and being like, "Woo-hoo, look at these!" But Sam, for some reason, seemed to want to share them only with these filthy rocker-type guys who looked like they'd never taken a shower in their lives. I would be like, "Seriously, Sam, how could you go near those guys? Shouldn't you at least hose them down first? De-louse them? Something?"

I, on the other hand, had the good sense to be attracted only to the guido type of guys I'd grown up with at the shore—the kind who were half muscle, half hair gel, and about a half step away from some serious 'roid rage. What could possibly be a more attractive combination than anger and back acne, all doused in a generous spraying of Drakkar Noir?

Partying in Dayton wasn't quite like partying in Jersey. For one thing, we'd often head out to Kentucky for nightlife, which should tell you a little something about what Ohio had going on. Kentucky had this bar where you'd put on a Velcro suit and jump off a ledge onto a wall that you'd stick to. And you'd do this for fun.

My first time in Kentucky, some guy heard me speak and said, "You're a Yankee." I was like, "What are we talking about here? The Civil War? The baseball team?" I had no idea that people even *thought* that way anymore. Besides, I didn't know what to call him back, because I didn't know what the opposite of a Yankee was. Rebel? Cracker? Braves fan? I wasn't sure which one he'd prefer. Learning about foreign cultures was so confusing. But that's what going to college is all about: becoming a more well-rounded person. And speaking of well-rounded . . .

I would go back home for semester breaks, each time heavier than the last. I stretched the freshman fifteen into the freshman twenty-five. It was the only part of college where I was an overachiever. I remember taking a bus home once and waiting for my parents to pick me up at Dunkin' Donuts. I came walking out of there with a box of Munchkins, and my dad took one look at me and said, "Put down the donuts." It was like a hostage situation: "Let go of the chocolate glazed and no one gets hurt. I don't want to see one drop of jelly spilled." So much for being happy to be home.

It's not like I didn't realize I was piling on the pounds. I mean, Christ, we had mirrors in the dorm rooms. But some of the girls there also had a healthy dose of denial going on. One night Nancy, Sam, and I were strutting through the ghetto, looking for some college guys to meet.

Nancy asked us, "Does this dress look too tight on me? I don't want to look like an overstuffed sausage." Apparently, looking like a regular sausage was just fine.

Sam reassured her, "No, you look great. How about me? Do you think these jeans are too tight?"

Finally I'd had enough of their mutual enabling and flat-out lies. "Girls, let's face it: we're getting fat. We're goddamn huge. I mean, what did you expect, living on a diet of alcohol and Doritos? And the only exercise we get is running to the toilet to puke. So we can either give that up or we can keep squeezing ourselves into our clothes and carry on."

We carried on.

When Sam and I moved out of the dorms, we lived in the off-campus housing known as "the dark side" (it was either that or "the ghetto"). We had a cemetery at the end of our street, and that was where we'd go rollerblading or walk off the seventy thousand calories we'd managed to consume the night before.

The girls in Dayton didn't seem overly conscious about their weight. No one there was going to be confused for a runway model (unless the kind of runway we're talking about involved jumbo jets), but we didn't seem to have the anorexia and bulimia so in fashion on other school campuses. In fact, let's just say that any one of us could've driven my Malibu with the COW license plate and it wouldn't have been all that much of an overstatement.

When one of my sisters, who is very attractive and has a great shape, came to visit me at school, we walked through a field where the lacrosse players were practicing. The entire team stopped what they were doing and started to clap. I had already put on the pounds, so I knew the applause wasn't for me. Besides, I had walked that way during practice before hoping to get picked up—or at least get a phone number, a cat call, a "hey, show us your tits." Anything . . . I mean, how many dozens of times does a girl have to walk back and forth across a friggin' field to get a little attention?—but I never got a response. I think the players were actually in shock at seeing a thin, good-looking blonde.

My excuse for my weight gain was that the food at college was amazingly awesome. We went to TGI Friday's for breakfast, lunch, and dinner. I had a declining balance on my food card but felt that I ate like a queen (if queens feast on jalapeño poppers). After a few months at school, my face was so round you could only see the slits of my eyes. To this day, I still wonder whose clothes I was wearing because there is no way in hell mine could have fit. All I know is that the first time I came home from school, I had to raid my sisters' closets—of course, everything was very long on me, so I looked like I had become Amish, but at least I had something to wear.

My weight was not the worst of it. My parents also had a fit because my friend Jenn, who had failed out of Dayton, would bleach my hair blonde each semester. When the lights were out, you could see it giving off a faint glow. It was like a really subtle shade of uranium.

The second I got home, my mom would be there with her plastic gloves on, greeting me at the door like a deranged germophobe, ready to dye my hair in our kitchen to her favorite shade of ash brown—I think the hair color matched our kitchen cabinets perfectly. (Maybe that's what gave my mom the inspiration. I guess I should be happy it wasn't the linoleum.) The best part about it was that my mother could never dye my hair without burning my scalp. Her hands were protected under layers of plastic, immune to the scalding heat of the chemicals. I'd be wearing a garbage bag over my body to catch any toxic fallout, while the skin on my scalp burned away.

Sometimes she'd have her friend's daughter, who was in beauty school at the time, come over and give me a horrible perm. I looked like an unhappy poodle. That may explain why she went on to be a pet groomer, where undoubtedly her clients were more appreciative of her skills. I hated that egg smell of the chemicals, but at least it explained why we were doing this in the kitchen and not in the bathroom like normal people. I think my mother wanted to fool my father into thinking that for once she had actually cooked an omelet.

After the abuse—I mean beauty treatment—I was always sullen, even though I knew the horrible curls and the bald patches were just temporary, since I'd have my hair bleached again once I got back to Ohio. It's amazing, with that kind of treatment, that I had any hair left at all.

Another big part of looking good in college was tanning before a frat party. I can still smell the crisply frying skin, visualize the glamour of the eye goggles (the same kind we wore during experiments in science lab, which should have tipped me off that I shouldn't be doing this to my body), and remember the feeling of taking a nap in the tanning bed, lying naked in a pool of sweat—mine mixed with whoever's was there before me.

Sure, I was still stuck in the middle of friggin' fat-ass Ohio, but if I closed my eyes and felt my skin soak up the fake, cancer-causing rays, for a moment I could feel like I was truly home.

# 11

# "Meating" the One

There was more to college than fun, games, empty calories, and early stage skin cancer. There was the academic side to consider. And, truth be told, I considered myself to be doing quite well when I got a 0.7 GPA my first semester. Really, I thought that wasn't too bad for someone who never went to class. It was like I somehow managed to find a way to earn seven-tenths of a point just for getting out of bed on occasion, which I figured must have meant I was utterly brilliant—until my sisters told me I was going to screw up my life and end up working in Mom's florist shop forever.

That did it! I brought my grades up out of sheer panic. Scared straight. Forget getting on the dean's list or into any kind of honor society; the idea of working in the florist shop forever was all the motivation I needed.

Class work was easy, for the most part, if I could pay attention to it. But it was hard to keep my attention from wandering to the guys. They were like horny, little lab rats running through a maze of frat houses, fueled by hormones and cheap malt liquor.

I managed to nab one of these fine specimens for myself. He was beefed up. On steroids. A real meathead. Everything Jerry the Plumber had warned me about.

In other words, he was perfect.

How I managed to find the one musclehead from Miami who looked like a guido that escaped from the Jersey shore, I'll never know. (I was like a guido magnet; it's as if they were ensnared by my Volumaxx and couldn't get out.) And how he managed to end up in the Midwest—or in college at all—is another unsolved mystery. But what I do know is that I saw all the red flags . . . and not only did I do nothing to avoid them, I ran straight at them like a bull. Honestly, I couldn't have been more attracted to him if the steroid needle had still been hanging out of his ass cheek.

I remember how I met him—mostly. Parts of that night are a complete blur. I had another partner in crime who loved to party as much as I did. Kristy was from Long Island (we would later move to New York together), another blonde with high hair. We looked like sisters. In fact, she'd use my sister's fake ID. (I'm not sure why she didn't just get her own fake ID . . . but then, I'm not sure we were ever sober enough to question it.) Anyway, one night at a bar called Tim's, we met two juniors. One of them asked Kristy to go to a frat party. So I thought, *What the hell? Let me ask his big guido friend over there if he'll bring me.* There's nothing like being forward and confident—and, yes, drunk—to boost your social life. So that was how our two-year relationship started.

Mr. Meathead was dynamic. He was in a wild fraternity that threw the best dances (an important quality when selecting a life partner). He worked hard and he played hard. No . . . wait. I mean he worked *out* hard and he played hard. As for a job, he was a camp counselor in the summer. And to make that even sexier, his mother had gotten him the job.

He was also very protective—and, by that, I mean clinically insane. God forbid anyone ever looked at me; that was when the fights started. It was like having a rabid pit bull as a bodyguard. I swear he'd have started a fight with a near-sighted eighty-year-old if he'd thought he was glancing my way: "What are you looking at? Yeah, you! With the thick glasses! And the cane! I saw you checking out my girl!"

To add to the low-key image he had going, my guido also drove a car with tinted windows and Florida plates. Maybe inconspicuous in Miami, but not in the Midwest. It was like Scarface took a wrong turn and ended up in the middle of *Field of Dreams*.

But I will say this for Mr. Meathead: since he was two years older than I was and wanted to apply to law school (so he could someday represent himself in court and save on lawyer fees, he joked . . . I mean, I think he joked), he was a great help with my schoolwork. He was also a bit of a romantic. We had our special place to eat out, which was Denny's, and if we ever wanted a getaway from his frat house—which kind of felt like a conjugal visit at a state prison, only less hygienic and with more porn magazines stashed under the mattresses—he would take me to stay at the Marriott by the mall and we'd swim in the indoor pool. I guess that was the closest thing Dayton had to South Beach and the Jersey shore—at least once *we* got there.

During the summer he would visit me in my natural habitat of New Jersey, and I'd drive down to see him strut around Miami. One year he even flew me out to meet him, then drove me back to college. I remember thinking he was a real man because he didn't pull over to sleep at the truck stops. Little did I realize he was so 'roided up, he probably could have sprinted to Ohio with me on his back. It would've saved us some money on gas and tolls. Plus I wouldn't have had to hear the Beatles the whole way there. You'd think a musclehead like him would have been more "Happiness in Slavery" than "I Wanna Hold Your Hand," but there you go. He could surprise me.

That was evident the time we went to Daytona Beach in Florida for spring break and he—at six-foot-one—decided it would be a good idea to tackle me—all of five-foot-one—in the ocean. I ended up spraining my ankle and leg and got off the plane on crutches. When my parents met me at the airport, they weren't mad at him; no, they were pissed at me because I had to work at the florist shop and my injuries might slow me down. If I had been in a full-body cast, they probably would have had me de-thorning roses with my teeth.

Once, when he came to visit the florist shop, I asked him to go on a delivery and he thought it would be dangerous. Apparently, in Miami, pizza guys and other delivery people were regularly robbed or killed. Okay, so I get that there are times when you might actually feel like you could kill someone for a pizza—I've had those pepperoni cravings, too— but who would shoot somebody for a funeral arrangement? The irony alone would be too much to bear. So it was up to me and old man Art to keep doing the deliveries. Mr. Meathead was not as macho as I'd thought.

My mother was not overly impressed. Believe it or not, she was actually worried I would end up getting married to him and move to Florida. It didn't seem to worry her that I was already going to college a few states away. Nor did it seem to concern her too much that her daughter was dating a juiced-up gorilla who looked like he'd been banned from the World Wrestling Federation for aggression issues. Nope, my mom had only one worry, and this was it: I would marry him and live far away, which to her meant not within walking distance.

Though I had no intention of marrying him—I mean, I wasn't *that* stupid—things did get pretty serious between us. I knew he was committed to me when I saw two toothbrushes in his bathroom. I thought buying me a toothbrush meant one of two things: either he loved me or I had really bad morning breath. Optimist that I am, I went with the first.

But the problem was that my meathead partied a little too hard, and his personality became more aggressive over time. Not in a "oh, yeah, that's hot, take me now" kind of way, but more in a "the restraining order says fifty feet, not forty-nine" sort of way. He also had this weird sense of humor, which involved practical jokes, like hiding from me when we were at the airport. One minute he'd be standing next to me, and the next he'd be gone and I'd have to go look for him like some kind of overgrown kindergartener playing hide and seek.

Eventually things just stopped working between us. Talk about awkward. Right after we broke up, we still had to take our final exams—mine for the semester and his forever, since he was a senior by then. We actually had to sit next to each other in one class during the test. And the worst part of it was that I couldn't ask to cheat off him.

Then, just like that, the guy who used to hide at airports suddenly disappeared. He graduated and I never heard from him again.

Jerry the Plumber had been right: I got through the relationship just fine. It was the breakup that was a bitch.

He had been my first serious boyfriend since high school. Now he was gone from my life and, more importantly, so were his muscles. And there I was, alone, afraid, and facing a future of uncertainty and soul-wrenching desperation.

Well, not really. But I was facing another summer of having to go back and work at my mom's florist shop, and that kind of sucked, too.

Or so I thought. . . .

# 12

# Semester Break(up)

What could be better for getting over a breakup than working at my mother's florist shop? Arranging flowers to deliver to happy wives or girl-friends from their loving husbands or boyfriends (or sometimes from both on her birthday)? It was my own personal hell. My version is filled with carnations and baby's breath, along with someone who looks and sounds a lot like my mother, continually saying, "Lauren, what's wrong with you? What are you, crazy? Who puts a red rose next to a red carna-tion?" and prodding me with her pitchfork.

To make things worse, this was not a fast-food chain, where you could spit in a customer's food if you were unhappy with your own life. There was nothing for me to do but throw myself into my work, such as it was. I'd been working in my mother's shop since I was ten, so I could wrestle carnations, roses, daisies, baby's breath, and their brethren into picture-perfect bouquets and funeral wreaths of breathtaking beauty in mere minutes. I was starting to get worried that I might not be suited for anything else.

Mom didn't help matters, of course. She'd always say that with my experience there, "You'll always have a career." I could travel the globe and find work with any florist in the world. And who wouldn't want that for their child? Other mothers dreamed of their kids becoming doctors and lawyers. Mine visualized me somewhere in rural China, arranging flowers into the shape of a dragon's head twenty hours a day for the respectable wage of ten cents a week. That would have been part-time work compared to the hours I pulled in my mom's shop.

Had I worked every Christmas since I was ten years old? Yes. Every Easter? Yes. Could I make flower arrangements for a funeral or wedding with my eyes closed? Yes . . . and sometimes I actually did. That was the only time I could take a rest.

But those weren't the only skills I picked up working for the family business. There were other, maybe less "transferrable" skills. The Passaic River ran directly behind the shop, and when the water was high, the rats would scurry to dry ground—such as the flower shop's basement. Our basement was the Grand Central Station of the rodent world, and I was the lone custodian. When the fucking things died down there, it was my job to go in with a bucket and a shovel, pick them up, and throw their stinking, dead bodies away. Yes, it was a glamorous life I led. And yes, I believe that was exactly how the Black Plague had started.

The basement of the florist shop had a secret dungeon. That was the room where boxes and boxes of flowers were delivered and where I lined up buckets of water to cut them in. Then I brought them upstairs to the refrigerators. I'm not taking about one or two boxes of flowers either. I'm talking about twenty boxes or more from all over the world. I had to de-thorn the damn roses from South America with a huge machete that could easily have cut off all my fingers (believe me, you could tell who our new workers were from the number of stitches they had to get). To this day, I don't want to set foot in South America. In fact, when someone talks about the rainforest being destroyed, I'm fine with it if that's where all the friggin' roses come from.

I hated Valentine's Day most of all. My fingers were constantly cut up and covered with blood. Yeah, like some guy would really want to put a ring on that.

When I first headed off to college, I couldn't wait to strike out on my own and find a job for myself. And where did I choose to go for employment? Directly to a goddamn florist.

This florist shop was something special. It was owned by two gay guys, and they had a crazy Asian driver. Sometimes the driver's wife would come looking for him, and he'd have disappeared with one of the owners for a couple of hours in the van. I imagine quite a few deliveries were made, none of which had anything to do with flowers. It was like one of those Spanish soap operas, where everybody was sleeping with everyone else behind each other's back, only there was no Spanish. All I cared about was watching where I stepped in the back of that delivery van.

I stayed at that florist's shop until it closed down. I came back from a school break my sophomore year to find the place boarded up like a crack house. After that, I decided to try something a little different, and I went to work at the gift shop at the Marriott—the same hotel where my ex and I used to go to get away from it all. Too much baggage. I left soon after I started and went on to PBJ Sport, a manufacturing company that made themed clothing. I considered it my first corporate job; it even came complete with an employee discount. So when I headed home for Christmas break, everyone got these sports-themed shirts as presents. That was the best part—the reactions on my family's faces. The worst part was trying to figure out discounts when we had sales. I remember calling Sam in a panic to see if she knew how to take 10 percent off. She, in turn, had to call her brother. It didn't say much for the math classes we were taking.

As part of my curriculum for my Bachelor of Science degree, I also had to do several hours of volunteer work at a children's daycare. When my group of kids started singing "Ninety-Nine Bottles of Beer on the Wall," I was not exactly handed an award for Volunteer of the Year (though, to be fair, I tried to change the lyrics to "ninety-nine stuffed animals on the wall" but these kids were purists and stuck to the original; also, I wasn't the one who'd started singing it in the first place—it was a wise-ass little three-year-old). Anyway, it was a crazy daycare center where the kids outnumbered the students/adults by a long shot, and someone always seemed to be getting stuck inside the toilet bowl (the kids, I mean; for the most part, that hardly ever happened to us adults). Suddenly, the family business didn't look so bad.

Once Mr. Meathead and I broke up, I kind of looked forward to coming home. For one thing, instead of driving home, I actually got to fly, which was always a special treat for me. I never got a direct flight; there was always a layover at Columbus or some other city I'd only vaguely heard of that separated me from New Jersey. Then, on the way back, I'd have to have my parents drive me to Islip, Long Island, because the flight never left from anywhere near my home; with what we spent in gas and tolls to get to the airport, I probably could have booked a direct flight but, as I've mentioned, math was not my strong suit.

For the times when I didn't fly back, I would try to carpool with someone listed on the travel board at school, which meant either having a passenger in my car to share gas costs and driving time or hitching a ride with somebody I'd never met. It was a good way to save money, protect the environment, and potentially get raped.

Once I got a ride home with a hippie couple who was headed to the girl's house in New Jersey. They were doing all the driving; my job was just to pay for gas, sit in the back, and sleep. My plan was to have Michelle pick me up for the weekend in Atlantic City without my parents having any idea I was in town. Unfortunately, they were both so stoned that the drive took forever, and we ended up stopping at the boy's house instead. His mother was so excited to have her son home from school, but she was obviously disappointed in his girlfriend. That night, the hippie girl and I—who were complete strangers—had to share a bed. She was clearly in love with her boyfriend, but she looked at me and said, "I feel as though his mother wishes you were the girlfriend instead." I wanted to say, "Well, yes, maybe because I don't have dreadlocks down to my ass and a ring through my nose. But trust me, your boyfriend is so not my type. I like boys who shower." But I didn't. I was still hoping we'd make it to Jersey and I could see Michelle and possibly hook up with a boy from home without my parents ever knowing. The next day, we got such a late start, we ended up just driving back to Ohio. Guess that hook-up just wasn't meant to be.

The few times I did fly home with my friend, Nancy, it was always the same: Nancy would have her parents there at the airport, greeting her with Santa hats on and all ready for their holiday at the Plaza in New York, while I was on the pay phone giving Art the location of where to pick me up at the curb in front of the gate. So yes, I'd say my friends and I had different types of breaks . . . and normally I couldn't wait to get back to school and relax.

During a break between semesters, I was back again where I belonged, stuck in the basement of my mom's florist shop, cleaning up rat carcasses and slowly bleeding out through the many cuts in my fingers. I figured one day, about twenty years from then, someone would find my lifeless, exsanguinated body down in that basement, half-eaten by rats and clutching a single South American rose in one hand.

But that was before *he* walked in and saved me from spinsterhood at the ripe old age of twenty.

# 13

# Melt with You

———

He was tall and handsome. He was well-dressed, with a definite presence about him. He walked into the florist shop and saw me standing with my mother behind the counter.

"Oh, he must be here looking for your sister, Josephine," Mom whispered.

*Oh, of course. Thanks for the vote of confidence*, I thought. *I'll just go in back and slit my wrists with the rose shearers now.*

But the truth was it was impossible to tell exactly who he was there for. He was the kind of guy who could be flirting with anyone in the room, from little girls to little old ladies. He was all charm.

I had seen him at the florist many times, and I had come to think of him as Mr. Melt, because that's exactly what my heart did every time I saw him. (I suppose I could have also called him Mr. Nauseated, because that was how he made my stomach feel, or Mr. Sweat, because I seemed to perspire a lot around him, but those don't have quite the same ring to them.) Mr. Melt had been a steady customer of ours for several months, since he'd bought the funeral home across the street. As my mother, the eternal romantic, put it, "People are always dying, so he'll never run out of business. That means he's a good catch."

But my interest in him wasn't *that* shallow. He was male-model mate-rial and looked a lot like JFK, Jr. He exuded confidence, seemed to love attention, and was well put together in the sort of Brooks Brothers/Polo preppy crap my dad always liked and wanted me to wear (like there's something wrong with Lycra!). For a change, he wasn't my stereotypical guido. He wore shirts with actual sleeves. He addressed me as Lauren rather than "yo." Sure, it would take some getting used to. But I was will-ing to make an exception.

I'd known him since my last break from school, but we'd both been dating other people. This time, though, my mom was wrong. This time he'd come looking for me.

It didn't take us long to get together, although I have to admit at first it all seemed a little like a cheesy rom-com to me—the girl who worked in the florist shop met the guy who owned the local funeral home. I could just see the tagline: "Their customers may die, but their love never will." The funeral home was where he first asked me out. Romantic, right? I was dropping off a delivery, and he asked if I wanted to go out on Friday night. I said yes, but then we both realized it was already Friday. Both of us worked all week during the summer, so the days tended to blur together. I swear his was like the White Castle of funeral homes: it never closed. Plus everything was put into a square-shaped box.

He picked me up that evening, and we went to a nearby Charlie Brown's. I was afraid there'd be some initial awkwardness. Me: "Mmmm . . . what's that cologne you're wearing?" Him: "Cologne? Oh, that's for-maldehyde. Hard to wash off." But there wasn't. In fact, the only source of stress came from me. He didn't know how old I was because, back when we'd first met, I hadn't even been of drinking age, but I'd lied and told him I was a year older and was just finishing school late, because what guy can resist an academically challenged, unambitious girl? He was almost seven years older than I was, and I wanted to appear more worldly and mature. What better way to do that than by lying to his face?

Don't get me wrong; I've always been into older guys. When Michelle and I were preteens on the beach, I'd ignored the scrawny boys our own age and checked out the buff lifeguards who were ten years older. Forget the fact that I was so flat at that age they could have used me as a surf-board. I'd really thought I could get one of them to go after me if I tried—and I don't just mean by drowning.

So I'm not sure what was wrong with me that night I went out with Mr. Melt, but I had two strong drinks and spilled my guts to this near-stranger. Maybe it was the feelings I had for him. Maybe it was the smell of the embalming fluid making me dizzy. But I told him practically my whole life story—except for the part about my age; that I kept from him for another year or so. Finally, when the truth came out, he couldn't have cared less. It was my parents who were relieved that they could go back to putting the right number of candles on my birthday cake. I swear, they were ready to crack under the pressure and tell him my age, my Social Security number, and anything else he wanted to know.

After we started dating seriously, I had to go back to school to finish my junior and senior years, but we kept up a long-distance relationship. That was when "long-distance" also described the types of phone calls we made—none of this free Skype or instant messaging. I spent most of the money I made on phone bills, but Mr. Melt was nice enough to send me airline tickets to fly all over the country so I could go to his friends' weddings with him on weekends. Without my parents knowing, of course. They'd have thrown a shit fit if they'd found out I was doing the Macarena at some country club in California instead of doing my homework. Once, in a pure coincidence, we ended up on the same flight as his aunt and uncle, and we had to duck down in our seats the entire time so they wouldn't report back to my parents. And forget going to the bathroom!

Other than my bladder nearly bursting, things were going really well with Mr. Melt. He was having some seriously positive effects on my life. Because I hated being away from him, I started taking more credits each semester and graduated from college in only three and a half years—with honors. Not bad for someone whose biggest honor before that was winning first place in a beer-chugging contest.

And, because we spent so much time at his country club, he introduced me to golf, which would come in handy later when I entered the corporate world and took clients out on the course. (I was actually quite good, and most of the time those client outings would be fun, but sometimes I'd have to keep reminding myself that I just had to survive nineteen holes—eighteen holes of golf and one asshole I had to be nice to the whole time.)

But, while our courtship seemed picture-perfect from the outside, there was something strange about the whole thing. I went from living in *Animal House* to living *The Stepford Wives* really quickly—too quickly—without even undergoing hypnosis or whatever Tom Cruise did to Katie Holmes. The point is that I felt like that same little girl again, trying to escape her life by getting on *The Love Boat*.

Little did I know it would come crashing into *Fantasy Island* at full speed ahead—without my life jacket.

# 14

# Finding Work and Getting Stoned

———

It was 1992 when I graduated, and it was tough to find a job. I wanted to help pay for a wedding that would never be, so I was pretty desperate to find work immediately. Not "going back to my mother's florist shop" kind of desperate, but maybe just a step or two away from selling my eggs to a nice, infertile couple.

Anyway, my eggs were spared because my mother's friend's daughter's company had an opening for $18,500; I was living at home at the time, so I could survive on that amount. I went to work for Curtin Matheson, a medical supply company, though I'm pretty sure my parents thought I was working for a curtain store: "Curtain who? How come I never heard of them? And why don't you get us any discounts on drapes?"

I was an assistant sales rep for pharmaceuticals, so basically our salespeople from Pennsylvania to Long Island treated me like their own personal slave. It seemed that, in their world, "assistant" and "servant" were synonymous. Medical reps are a bunch of conceited assholes anyway.

They walk around like they're the surgeons rather than the glorified drug pushers they are. I mean, hanging around a hospital doesn't exactly make you George Clooney in *ER*.

My job mostly entailed sitting on my ass all day. I would spend hours at my desk, on the phone with clients, sales reps, and medical staff. A good day was when I got to go to the hospitals to see the clients. I figured the worst I could get was walking pneumonia from being around sick people in the waiting room, which was still better than getting secretarial spread. At least with walking pneumonia, there's some walking involved. Maximum-security prisoners probably get more exercise time than I did. Between the sitting and scarfing down oily, cheesy pizzas and calzones during my thirty-minute lunch break, this was a sure-fire recipe for disaster.

And sure enough, after several months of this routine, I got really sick one day as I was sitting at my desk, and I thought I was having a heart attack. The only thing wrong with my self-diagnosis was that the pain wasn't in my heart; it was in my lower back. (Proof positive that working for a medical company really does not make you a doctor.) It felt like I had been kicked in the back by a horse and I couldn't breathe. I broke out in a sweat, so I got up and went to the bathroom to pour cold water on my face. That helped a little, so I went back to work, never thinking, *Duh, I work at a medical supply company. Maybe we have something stronger than cold water.*

That evening it happened again when I was sleeping. The pain was so bad, I woke up and screamed for my parents. They were so shocked by my screams that now *they* were convinced they were having heart attacks. (No mystery about where the hypochondria comes from . . .)

My father came running into my bedroom with the Merck medical manual that sat next to him on his nightstand like a Bible. This was the low-tech version of WebMD, but the basic idea was the same: whatever you read convinced you that you were dying.

After consulting the manual, my father's first educated guess was that I was having my period. That's great, Dr. Quincy, Medical Examiner, but wouldn't I be bleeding? Then he decided it was my appendix, but the pain was on the wrong side. We went down the list alphabetically—"Alzheimer's?" "No." "Arthritis?" "No." "Asperger's syndrome?" "No."—until we reached scurvy. But since I wasn't a pirate and

I'm pretty sure no one's had scurvy since the seventeenth century, I felt pretty safe rejecting that one.

I told them it had happened at work, and after I had walked a little it didn't feel as bad. So my parents had me walk and walk and walk around the house, which didn't make it any better, but it did give me some understanding of what it's like to be my mother and never sit still. After that, the pain actually got worse, and even though I had to pee, I couldn't.

That was it! We were off to Saint Joseph's Hospital in Paterson, one of the most renowned areas in New Jersey for medicine—if by "medicine" you mean crack and heroin. Going back to the hospital where you were born is always a little weird; it was like my parents were bringing me in under warranty. "Look, we've only had this one for about twenty-three years and she's already defective. Any chance we can trade up?"

Anyway, we went all the way to Paterson and spent a few fun hours in the emergency-room waiting area—our companions mostly stabbing and shooting victims, which gave a nice feel to the whole experience—just to find out that I had a "small" kidney stone that was stuck. The doctor told me that I should be able to pass it if I drank enough water.

"That's it? Drink water?" my mother said to the doctor. It was as if she was disappointed I didn't need surgery. "I mean, we came all the way here in the middle of the night. Can't you just slice her open and check? Our insurance will cover it."

The water actually worked. After about ten gallons, the kidney stone moved and I was able to pass it. But it was as sharp as razor blades, and it felt more like a boulder than a stone.

After the announcement that I'd be able to pass it by drinking water, he imparted more good news. Apparently, I had a "family" of kidney stones taking up residence in my body. He helpfully explained that some people just seem to produce these stones—sort of like having my own private rock quarry stuck up my urinary tract.

It turned out that doctor was right. My kidney stone family, who I like to think of as Sly and the Family Stone, grew to about twenty. That's the number of stones I've passed in twenty years. I'm hoping the next one is more of a precious stone, maybe an emerald or a ruby—something nice that I can make a necklace out of. I'm doing Kegel exercises to add some pressure, like they do with coal to turn it into diamonds. Then maybe I can sell my own jewelry line on QVC like Joan Rivers. After so many medical visits throughout the years, I had gotten a lot of advice. One doctor told me, "Just drink two beers a night. It will help you pee." Needless to say I stuck with this doctor, whom I believe got his PhD at the prestigious Heineken University.

To slow the production of kidney stones, he also told me I needed to stay away from cheese—the food group that made up about 80 percent of my diet when I was working at Curtin Matheson—as well as a whole list of my other favorite foods, and get some regular exercise. So pizza lunches and a sit-down job weren't for me. It was time for something new. My eyes were on Manhattan.

# 15

# Meltdown

———

Did you ever notice how some people have that fake laugh? There's sort of a ten-second delay and then they realize they're supposed to be laughing—but aren't—at something that's supposed to be funny—but isn't—so then they overcompensate by making a noise that sounds like they're saying the syllables "hahaha." I mean, who actually laughs like that?

To fit into Mr. Melt's world, it was important to have that kind of fake laugh for social events, dinner parties, weddings, and all types of country-club affairs.

I didn't have that laugh.

Don't get me wrong. I'm the kind of person who loves to laugh. Once, at a restaurant with friends, I laughed so hard, I vomited into a cloth napkin. So while I can puke and laugh simultaneously (which is quite a party trick, not to mention damn attractive), I can't seem to fake laugh no matter how hard I try.

I didn't try very hard.

While I was in Mr. Melt's world, with his friends, I felt like a fish out of water . . . just didn't belong with his polished, preppy crowd. But when we were alone at his house on the couch watching *Melrose Place*, he was great. If a couple's problems can't be solved by watching *Melrose Place*, they don't have a chance. We definitely had a chance.

The other problem was that Mr. Melt always wanted to be the center of attention. It was like I adored him and he adored . . . himself. When we were out, I always hoped a guy would come over and flirt with me, but it never happened. Nope. Not once. I would've settled for a busboy accidentally brushing against my boob when he cleared the table. Nada. So on Mr. Melt's part, there was absolutely no jealousy whatsoever. But with me, he'd keep talking about all these girls in the room and how they all loved him.

So whenever I got him out in public, all my insecurities came out. Instead of feeling like a hot, petite blonde next to him, I felt like a dwarf with a bad dye job. If this was *Fantasy Island*, I was Tattoo waving at the plane, standing next to the distinguished Mr. Roarke. (Side note: if fantasies really did come true there, did nobody ever wonder why Tattoo wasn't a good three feet taller?)

I'm not saying Mr. Melt acted like a bad guy. He was programmed to be a gentleman: he stood up from the table when I got up and all that good stuff you learn in finishing school or in movies about gorgeous preppies who turn out to be shallow losers. But there was something about him that wasn't quite human. He had the etiquette, but lacked emotion.

Still, that didn't stop me from accepting his proposal. He asked me to marry him right around Valentine's Day. I had a dream that it would happen. When I told him that, he said, "Well, let's make your dream come true" (which really is something Mr. Roarke, or an arrogant dick, would say). I was graduating college early and going home to be with him, so my girlfriends at school—classy chicks that they were—threw me an engagement party, for which they decorated a dorm room with condoms.

Our real engagement party was at a really nice restaurant—his choice, of course—because there wasn't enough room for everyone at my choice of venue, which was his couch. It was all very grand; no one blew up any condoms in lieu of balloons, and everybody knew about our engagement: the former mayor's daughter marrying the town's most eligible bachelor.

After that, I fantasized about the wedding and even went out and bought a dress, but I never saw us making it down the aisle. With all the premonitions I'd had, I couldn't actually picture us ending up together (which, in a way, *is* a kind of premonition, right?). As for Mr. Melt . . . well, he seemed still to picture himself as the town's most eligible bachelor.

When his best friend broke up with his girlfriend, the two of them started going to strip clubs together. I would always pretend it was okay with me, but it wasn't okay. I mean, seriously? What girl is like, "Yeah, babe, go have a good time. Make sure she grinds all over you. You know how I love it when you smell like a stripper!" He'd come back all drunk and happy, and say we should name our first girl Heather after this dancer he'd met. Yeah, that was a good idea. And then what—we'd shove dollar bills down her diaper to get her ready for her future career? It was almost like he was getting married just to have the bachelor party.

As for the marriage itself, it was clear he was having second thoughts. When the wedding got closer, he started pulling that "cold feet" shit. I would spend hours on the phone, crying and trying to get a straight answer out of him. It wasn't a pretty picture. Mascara streaming down my face. Snot running out of my nose. There was a reason I did this over the phone and not face to face.

Eventually my mom couldn't take it anymore.

"What's he talking about, he 'isn't sure'? The goddamn wedding's a few weeks away! We've got to let the caterers know if he's calling it off."

Seriously, Mom? The caterers? Yeah, I wouldn't want to inconvenience them by having my wedding canceled! She would actually sit next to me while I was having my meltdowns on the phone and coach me.

"Who cares how he feels? Ask him whether he wants to get married or not. It's a yes or no question."

The whole thing with Mr. Melt ended when I accused him of cheating on me, without any proof, I just said it . . . and he actually admitted to it! I couldn't believe it. I had gotten the idea from one of those lousy cop movies, where a perp with a guilty mind confessed—even though he didn't commit the crime in question—just to get less jail time. But the best was my dad's reaction. When I told him what had happened, he shrugged and said, "Every man makes mistakes before getting married."

*'Scuse me?* Clearly my father and I had very different definitions of "mistake." To me, a mistake was buying me carnations when I prefer

daisies; to my father it was going to sleazy strip clubs and dangling the wedding carrot in front of me.

The truth is my father was right: everyone does make mistakes before getting married. I made two. One was saying yes, and the other was trying to change myself to fit into somebody else's world. That was something I would never do again, no matter how amazing that world seemed from the outside.

It was not until I walked away from Mr. Melt that I found the real me once more. And wouldn't you know it? The real me was living in some dump in the West Village with Sam.

# 16

# Single in the City

───

The day after I broke off my engagement, I moved to Manhattan. It was time for a fresh start. I found an apartment in the ultra-cool West Village, which, despite its laid-back, artsy reputation, is one of the most expensive areas in the city. Which means you're going to pay roughly the same amount for a studio as you would for a 5,000-square-foot house in New Jersey. And all those hippie types you see sauntering about with pink Mohawks on their heads and guitars on their backs? They're singing on subway platforms and subsisting on weed and cans of tuna just to make rent. Basically you must be willing to live in a shoebox with, oh, about ten of your closest friends.

Or, in my case, one really kind and somewhat gullible one.

The first thing I did after signing the lease was call up my old college roommate, Sam, and beg her to move in with me. Well, "beg" isn't exactly the right word. More like "lied my ass off" to convince her that I'd found the perfect place.

"Sam, it's amazing. You should see the long hallways it has."

That was the truth. Kind of. The whole place was one long hallway! If you stood in the middle of the apartment and stretched out your arms to each side, you could touch both walls. But why quibble over such small details? I mean, what's a few square feet among friends? Close quarters can sometimes bring people closer together physically and emotionally. Look at prison inmates.

"Plus there's a back yard," I went on. Well, there was a restaurant behind us that had outdoor seating—as well as a potential rat infestation. But, as a survivor of the rat wars at the florist shop, I knew how to deal with rats. And I don't mean just my ex-fiancé.

Sam, trusting soul that she was, agreed to move in. I'm not sure she'd ever had a permanent address. She was like a cross between a hobo and that last tampon you find buried at the bottom of your purse: she would just drift around a while and then end up in exactly the right place when somebody needed her most.

For a while, living with Sam felt like being back at the college ghetto. But in New York, unlike Ohio, we were only a few blocks—and possibly one paycheck—away from the real ghetto. Since we didn't have much money, we lived on Chinese takeout. I'd have an egg roll for breakfast because it had the word "egg" in it. I'd ration out the food to make it last as long as possible, which meant the refrigerator was always filled with white cardboard boxes. They were stacked so high on top of each other it looked like I was trying to rebuild the Great Wall of China. Sam would always threaten me, "If that food's not gone by Friday, you're gonna find it under your pillow."

Sure enough, on Saturday morning I would wake up to the smell of week-old General Tso's chicken coming from my mattress, which for me meant breakfast in bed. Yet it smelled better than what Sam sometimes woke up with. She still hadn't gotten over her obsession with long-haired band guys—and, luckily for her, New York seemed to have an unending supply of them. The scuzzier, the better. I swear if the local homeless shelter had put together a musical group, Sam would've had more babies than even Angelina Jolie would know what to do with.

The living arrangement didn't exactly improve when my cousin, Anthony, stayed with us. Remember *Three's Company*? Well, I'm telling you three definitely *ain't* company. Jack, Janet, and Chrissy we were not. Three might be fun when you're doing shots at the Regal Beagle, but when you're rooming together in a five hundred square foot apartment— not so much.

It seems that while I'd been on the three-and-a-half-year college plan, Anthony had opted for the less-efficient, less-economical five-year plan, like he was leasing a damn Dodge. He'd started out at a school in Rhode Island but somehow ended up in North Carolina. Maybe because he had already dated all the girls this side of the Mason-Dixon. Anyway, wherever he was attending college, Anthony always had a dog. And I'm not talking about one of those small dogs you can fit in your carry-on bag. Anthony would always have a shedding, shitting, jumping, humping, slobbering type of huge dog. If it were a person, it'd be like that guy in *The Green Mile*. When I'd visit Anthony at school, he thought he was doing me some big favor by letting me sleep in his bed. But between the dog hair and the dog drool on the comforter (I assume it was dog drool . . .), it was just plain gross.

And when Anthony came to stay at the apartment, he brought the same disgusting comforter with him. I'd get up in the morning and find him on our couch, wrapped up in it like a foul-smelling cocoon. He didn't have the dog anymore, but who needs the dog when the comforter has that same dog stink? Anthony had been inside the dorm room of every girl in college, but apparently he'd never been inside a Laundromat.

Anthony didn't stay with me long. Caring cousin that I was, I found him a job pretty quickly at a computer company. Anything to get him out.

Even after he got his own place, we still hung out. We saw lots of crazy bands in the East Village, and had a great time. Or at least Sam and Anthony did. I would stand in the middle of whatever shithole they dragged me to with toilet paper wadded up in my ears like makeshift earplugs and look for the nearest fire exit. Sam and Anthony, on the other hand, thought these places were great. Before we went out, Sam would dress me so I'd look less South Jersey and more East Village. It worked, at least on the outside. On the inside, I was worried about touching anything for fear of contracting an STD. I'd only drink bottled beer because I was pretty sure these bars never washed the glasses, and I'd do a quick shot or two—enough to get me through the night, but not enough to make me have to use the ladies' room and squat over the toilet.

Once Anthony had left, our normal routine resumed. Sam would have all her eccentric friends over: heavy metal guys, artists, a few lesbian couples. Sam was in her whole groupie element at these shows, picking up unshowered guy after unshowered guy. We were both making salaries in the low twenties back then, so Sam and I would find the least-expensive restaurants to eat and drink beer in, though not necessarily in that order. In fact, never in that order. We'd drink first just in case the funds ran out. It didn't matter that we lived on the cheap; what mattered was that I was free—free of men for the first time in a long time, and free to explore New York as a young, single woman.

Sam and I would sometimes go to Moran's in the World Trade Center to mingle with the Wall Street guys and hopefully have them buy us drinks. Kristy, a friend from college, actually worked on Wall Street. Sam and I were freeloaders, and Kristy was our in with all those types of expense-account parties. She was always trying to set us up with her stockbroker friends, but we weren't buying into it. Sam cornered the market on dirtbag musician types, and I only invested in muscle-bound meatheads and egomaniacs, though I was giving the whole guy thing a break and just enjoying time with my girls.

Kristy and Meredith, who had also gone to Dayton, were roommates, and since they lived nearby, we hung out with them. Meredith was a teacher in the Bronx, which was about as glamorous as it sounds. At most schools three o'clock is known as dismissal time; at hers it was called "getting out early for good behavior."

Because Kristy was a well-paid Wall Streeter, their apartment was a step up from ours. You could probably fit our entire apartment inside their shower stall. Sam and I weren't exactly rolling in money, but we knew how to have a good time—that was the one thing (maybe the only thing) we'd all learned at Dayton. It was like we'd moved our college years into the city. We'd have Christmas parties with lights decorating the entire place, even in the bathroom (because who doesn't like to see their pee lit up in different colors?). We'd all meet after work for drinks at places like Boxer's or Down the Hatch, which were about as high-class as they sound and were potential recruiting grounds for Alcoholics Anonymous.

Often I would go to visit Kristy at her office on the eighty-ninth floor of the World Trade Center, and it would freak me out to be up that high in the clouds. I asked her, "Aren't you afraid to work up here?" and she told me that you get used to it. Anyway, I think that's what she said. I couldn't hear her because my ears were popping as we went to Top of the Six's for drinks on the rooftop.

Kristy had gone to college for communications, but gave that up to become a manager at Sandler O'Neill. She turned out to be a Wall Street genius, and as much as she always tried to get me to hook up with one of those trader types, she herself married her high school sweetheart, who, of course, was a penniless musician in a band with dreams of making it big.

She and I were both petite, blue-eyed blondes, and we'd get a lot of attention wherever we'd go, especially from guys who wanted to try it with "twins." We were both obsessed with makeup and would ask each other what one essential we would have on if we had no time to get ready and had to run out of a burning building. I said lipstick, and she said face powder because her skin was always shiny.

It breaks my heart to say this, but Kristy died in the World Trade Center attacks on 9/11. There are two things I'm sure of: One, that she is as happy and beautiful a presence in heaven as she was in our world. And two, that at the time, she was wearing face powder.

# 17

# Corporations, Computers . . . and Curry?

When I moved into Manhattan, I started selling air purification systems to keep the insides of buildings clean. Having worked in Curtin Matheson's stuffy office with piped-in, crappy air, I loved this new position and really believed in our products. I was like an enthusiastic Hare Krishna convert. I'm surprised I didn't shave my head and go on sales calls with a tambourine.

Since I sold our products all over the city, I would get subway tokens as a travel allowance. My company was on Thirty-Sixth Street between Fifth and Sixth Avenues. But I would walk all the way down to the South Street Seaport in lower Manhattan just to save the tokens for the weekend. Two great perks at this job: I was as thin as a rail, and our office had the best air quality in the city.

Another perk was the mechanic who would come with me to meas-ure and install the systems. His name was Billy, and he was a Guardian Angel (not like the people who died and passed over that I would some-times talk to, but like those big, bulky guys who tried to stop crime in the city while wearing berets); he also used to belong to a bunch of different street gangs and was now a Jehovah's Witness. Let's just say that between those three affiliations, Billy was pretty much the last guy you would ever want ringing your doorbell, but he was a great companion.

Billy and I would walk all over the city together, saving up tokens, and talk the whole time. He was only about twenty-four, but already had two kids, and he would tell me how he and his wife could only be intimate in one position because they were Jehovah's Witnesses. I learned a lot about that religion and what they could and could not do. Mostly it was "could not do."

I was the only woman working in the company selling those systems, so I got used to being exclusively around men. It was a real boys' club. My boss would have Howard Stern on in his office and constantly crack up at all the R-rated jokes, but I was already used to that from my father. (I wonder if they make Father's Day cards for that: "Thanks, Dad, for intro-ducing me to Howard Stern and his team of horny sidekicks and topless strippers at such a young age. It really helped with my career.") The guys at the company didn't treat me differently because I was a girl. Believe me, I knew all about air, but I was no airhead; I had to learn CAD program-ming, and they'd send me to sales calls at bars and pool halls, both places where the air was almost as filthy as the clientele—and where being a girl was actually a benefit. Most men wouldn't get halfway through their sales pitches there, whereas with me you'd think "air purification system" were suddenly the sexiest words that could ever be spoken.

The job was easy for me at first because we had just introduced a new system and all the leads we had were responses to our advertising. I just had to follow up. But the problem came with the pricing of the units. Most potential customers thought our products were amazing but didn't want to have to pay for air, which is normally free and can be found in abundance within our atmosphere.

The downside of the job was that the margins I would make on the systems I sold were very small. So while working in that type of clean-air environment was the real deal, I needed to go somewhere and make some real money. After all, a girl cannot live on air alone.

In New York, you meet a lot of strangers on public transportation . . . and each one is stranger than the next. For the most part, a city bus is like a psychiatric ward with wheels. So you try not to sit next to anyone, you try not to make eye contact, you try not to touch anything, for God's sake, and you definitely don't engage in conversation. Unless, of course, you're me. Then not only do you talk to strangers, but you take life-altering career advice from them.

I happened to meet a man on the bus when I was coming home from work one day, and he started asking me about what I do. When I told him I sold air purification systems, he said, "That's good . . . but you know, the future belongs to computers."

Okay. For a second I thought he was going to launch into a speech about how robots will someday take over the world. But instead, by the time we'd made it downtown, he had convinced me that working with computers was where the big opportunities were, along with the big money. He gave me the name of a computer consulting company; I gave them a call and they gave me a job. Who says New Yorkers aren't giving?

I went to work for an all-Israeli computer consulting firm and practically doubled my salary overnight. I loved the challenge of being in the new and developing field of technology—and the money didn't hurt either. Even the boss was great except for two things: he was a sexist pig and he refused to speak English. Okay, so maybe "great" isn't the right word. More like *meshuggah*.

Besides me, there were only two other women who worked in the company. And I could see why. In meetings, the boss would ignore us and speak Hebrew . . . except when he was referring to us as his "Charlie's Angels." That I understood. And didn't appreciate. I mean, for a girl who grew up on a steady diet of crappy TV shows, even I never wanted to be one of Charlie's Angels. Julie, Joanie, Laverne, Shirley, sure. But never an Angel. Maybe it had something to do with the hairstyles. I mean, an angel should have feathered wings, not feathered bangs. And who the hell was this Charlie anyway? Their pimp?

I lasted ten months at this consulting firm, until I was headhunted by our competitors. I quit via email that I sent to my boss while he was in Israel. I'm pretty sure he had some choice words for me in Hebrew, though "angel" probably wasn't one of them.

This was without a doubt the best career move I ever could have made—and I owed it all to some stranger on a bus. I was now ready to take stock tips from the woman sitting in the stall next to me in the ladies' room. This was freakin' fantastic!

When a new client would call, I was always asked to take it on. I was honest and had good intuition with people and projects—minus a few ex-boyfriends and that whole getting married thing. I even had the good sense to recruit the secretary from the air purification place to come to this new company with me.

At just twenty-three, I was dealing with human resources departments and managing directors and partners in different firms, from banks and pharmacies to Wall Street corporations. My job was to get the bid and oversee computer system deals that cost these companies millions of dollars to implement.

But it seems I still had a problem with percentages. There I was, a senior marketing rep, working and practically living in the World Trade Center, eating lunch at a different restaurant each day, wining and dining huge corporate clients—and I couldn't figure out how to leave a goddamn tip! I remember taking out an important client of ours; the president was there, the vice president, the commander in chief or whoever is next down the line. We went to a restaurant near Rockefeller Center, had dinner, had quite a few drinks, and charged it to my company card. I know I was a little tipsy, but I managed to add a tip and sign the receipt.

About a week later, my boss was going over the expense account. He was a great guy and wasn't upset about the big bill we'd racked up, but he said, "Lauren, let me ask you something. Do you know how to calculate a tip?" There I was once more, a college student back at the sports apparel store, calling up Sam to see how to deduct 10 percent for a sale. Turns out I'd left something like 50 percent for the waiters. So, once again, who says New Yorkers aren't giving? Especially the ones like me who suck at math.

To actually implement these computer systems we were selling, we had to hire computer tech people from all over the world, including Russia, China, and India. While I was killing it in the corporate world, bringing home commission checks for $20,000, what I was most proud of was that I changed so many lives by helping our workers become citizens. It wasn't always easy. Between handling visa and green card issues, I had to call my cousin, Anthony, for advice on how to have these guys pass drug tests with clean pee to get them into the country. After that, their pee was no longer my problem.

What *was* my problem—and the problem of anyone who worked in our office, or possibly the entire building, and had a functioning sense of smell—was that many of these international recruits had absolutely no sense of personal hygiene. So in addition to overseeing million-dollar jobs, I would have to give basic hygiene lessons to the employees, such as, "Wash your clothes if you wear them more than once," "Take a shower," and "Use deodorant." Some of the guys had some serious BO, and one of them had a constant farting problem so bad that the place always smelled like Indian curry. Spicy Indian curry. Spicy enough to make your eyes water if you were standing within a fifteen-foot radius. I swear that guy farted out tear gas. I can only imagine what it felt like for him coming out of his ass. I thought he was going to have to insert the fire extinguisher in places it was never meant to go.

For most women, "making it in a man's world" means climbing the corporate ladder. Being taken seriously in male-dominated field. Being invited to key meetings. Breaking the glass ceiling. For me, it meant lecturing men about cleaning their clothes, scrubbing their pits, and not farting in the presence of their coworkers or clients.

When I was not discussing the numerous benefits of Speed Sticks and Bean-o, I was putting together multimillion-dollar deals. It was the late nineties, and Y2K hysteria was in full bloom. I was responsible for finding programmers who were capable of switching computer systems to something that wouldn't bring business—and the planet—to a screeching halt. It was ridiculously tedious, totally crappy work, but companies like Goldman Sachs were willing to pay these guys—and me—a lot of money to make this happen. They may have started out making around $38,000 dollars, but within a year their salaries had climbed to $150,000 or more. Most of them already had a lot of experience working for CitiCorp, but I was still helping them achieve a level of prosperity they never would have had in their own countries. They worked their asses off and were so appreciative that I had found them and brought them to the States. It was an amazing feeling. It didn't hurt that I got a commission for every minute they worked.

I was very lucky: I was really good at my job and I loved it. So much that I practically skipped to the office every day. Soon, I had made enough money to move out of the apartment I was sharing with Sam and into a place of my own. (Sam, in the meantime, moved to a triple in the West Village.) Imagine my joy when I realized I could actually turn around in my living room without smacking my face into a wall. I also leased a shiny, red Acura (my first new car) and rented a parking spot in my building's garage (which, if you know Manhattan, is a pretty big deal). If you had asked me a few years earlier what I'd envisioned for my future, I probably would have told you about my plans for a depressing career in flower delivery. And spinsterhood. At least one of those wasn't going to happen now. Even with my career success, I was deathly afraid of turning into one of those women who never marries, adopts a bunch of cats, dies alone, and is only found after the cats have stripped the flesh from their bones.

There was a moment, though, when I thought the new Acura might be my ticket to romance. One day I was sitting in traffic on the highway when I saw a guy staring at me from the next car. I gave him the old sideways glance. *Not too bad.* And he looked like he wanted to ask me something. I casually rolled down the window and waited for him to chat me up before we started moving again.

"Hey, that's a hot car. How much does that run you?"

*He wants my lease information?* I rolled the window back up and pulled off the highway at the next exit. There was a CVS nearby, and I needed to pick up some Speed Sticks for the new guys at work.

# 18

# The Power of Prayer . . . and Hair

———

It has always amazed me how seemingly insignificant decisions can change the course of your life. Mine, for example: had I swum up rather than down when I was thirteen, I never would have died, gone to heaven, and come back able to communicate with the dead. If I hadn't spoken to that man on the bus, I never would have switched careers and gotten into computer consulting. And if I hadn't decided to go down the shore for an off-season night of drinking and dancing, I wouldn't have met my husband. Actually, I'd like to think we would have met anyway.

It was a chilly Saturday in April, and I was feeling antsy. It had taken a few months, but I was finally beginning to feel like my old self after the break-up with Mr. Melt. Which meant I wanted to go out, but not necessarily in the city. Because no matter how much I loved living and working in Manhattan, sometimes I just wanted to get away from it for a while. Say what you want about Jersey, but it's great to be able to jump in the car, cross a bridge or tunnel, and come out in a different world. Even better for me was that my parents had the shore house, and I decided to head down there for some drinking and dancing—after all, it had always cured what ailed me in the past.

I called my childhood friends Elissa and Kristen and told them to meet me. Like any good friends, they promised to be there for me in my time of need. I jumped in the Acura and was soon on the Garden State Parkway, just happy for the change of scenery.

The party doesn't really get started at the Jersey shore until after Memorial Day; until then it's as creepy as any ghost town. But I wasn't worried about finding something to do because there was always Jenkinson's. Jenk's is a pretty famous bar in Point Pleasant and pretty cool, too—that is, if you're into Springsteen cover bands, randy guidos, and sand in your tequila. Which, at the time, I was. It was a no-brainer—at least it would be a no-brainer after several drinks.

Jenk's did not disappoint: it was packed, and the band sounded almost as good as the Boss after a few drinks. Kristen, Elissa, and I had a blast in the way you can only with friends from back home. Especially since we ran into a bunch of guys we'd known forever but rarely got to see anymore. I hadn't had that much fun in a long time. I tried to hold on to that thought the next morning when I woke up with a rather nasty hangover. My head hadn't pounded like that since my college days in Dayton.

It was a Sunday morning down the shore. Off season and 8:00 a.m. Kristen and Elissa were still sleeping off the night before. There wasn't a whole lot to do, but I didn't feel like driving back to the city yet either. I opted for a walk on the beach. Given how hung over I was, it was probably more of a *stagger*.

Despite my raging headache and dry mouth, I couldn't help but notice that it was a beautiful morning. The sand looked pure and untouched after the long winter, and the early spring sun was warm on my face. I walked along the shore, breathing in the salty air. As I stared out at the gently rolling waves, words just came out of my mouth: "God, I just want to find a man who loves me as much as I love him." I was a little surprised at myself and looked around to see if anyone had heard. But no one was around, and if they had been, they probably would have been too drunk or hung over to care anyway.

Talking out loud made me realize my mouth felt like I'd eaten a bag of cotton balls. Wawa was close by, so I picked up a bottle of Snapple iced tea and downed it in one gulp. I still wasn't walking in a straight line as I headed back to Elissa's, but at least I wasn't going to die of dehydration.

That was when I heard this horrendous noise. I knew it was only a car, but in my condition it sounded—and felt—like a jackhammer at my temple. When I turned my head to look, I saw it was not only a sports car, but a Ferrari flying by me. "Are you kidding me, mister? It's waaaay too early for this noise."

I got back to Elissa's house, flopped down on a lounge chair outside, and closed my eyes. *This is great*, I thought. I could recover from the night before and get a base tan at the same time. But a few minutes later, there it was again. The jackhammer. I pulled myself up on my elbows just as it pulled into the driveway next door to Elissa's.

This guy climbed out. Even in my hangover haze, I couldn't believe what I was seeing. He looked like a refugee from the Ramones. Curly hair and long—almost down to his waist. Wearing a black wife beater and black shorts, and adorned with gold chains and bracelets. White high-top sneakers completed the look.

"Yo," I was tempted to say, "Seaside is five miles south of here."

If my head weren't splitting, I probably would have.

# 19

# More Than Meets the Ear

———

"You wanna see the house?" the Joey Ramone guy was asking me. Except it turned out his name wasn't Joey Ramone; it was Joe Pizza. And he had driven down the shore to check on the house he was building next door to Elissa's parents' place. Underneath the long hair and gold chains, I could see he had a kind, intelligent face.

"Why not?" I told him. I had nothing better to do, and I figured I would check it out, then report back to Elissa about what kind of person was moving in next to her parents.

So we went into his house and . . . well, not much happened at all.

There's no "love at first sight" moment here. First of all, I was hung over and not really in the mood for romance. Second, did I mention this guy looked like one of the Ramones? Not my usual type. At all. I was really just curious about the house.

I had a certain picture in my head about how this guy would decorate. I pictured some posters of Van Halen, and maybe Dee Snider hanging out on the couch, feet up on the coffee table, smoking a doobie.

But inside of an hour, this guy managed to shock the shit out of me—twice. First, as I said, when he got out of a Ferrari dressed like he was, and second, when I saw his house. It wasn't completely finished, but I could already see it was going to be classy. Not a cheesy metal poster anywhere. There was a large piano in the center of the main room.

Joe was talking a mile a minute, telling me how he worked in pharmaceuticals (which I found hard to believe was on the *legal* side) and that he was also a musician, which I found easy to believe. Sort of. Which is to say, I believed *he* believed he was a musician.

"Want to hear a song?"

I shrugged, thinking, *That's fine, as long as it's not anything really loud.*

He walked over to the piano, sat down on the bench, and began to play. Shock number three: this guy was really talented. And he was playing music for me. It suddenly struck me that I probably looked like I had been run over by a truck. I pulled a lipstick out of the pocket of my yoga pants and applied it quickly. Yes, I actually had lipstick on me.

People who know me know that I am never without lipstick. But Joe didn't know me yet. Joe looked over at me that morning, saw the lipstick, and got *the look* on his face. I knew that look because I'd seen it on plenty of other guys' faces. He was thinking, *She's putting on lipstick for me. This has possibilities.*

And I giggled to myself. Little did he know I'd put on lipstick before running out of a burning building.

# 20

# The Streets of New York

After that weekend down the shore, I started spending a lot of time with Joe. He was living in Hackensack, New Jersey, but he came to see me in the city all the time. He was always at least an hour and a half late, which of course drove me absolutely bat shit. I mean, he would get to Manhattan at like 9:30 or 10 o'clock at night. After I had worked all day. Most of the time, I could barely keep my eyes open by the time he got there. He went to work at whatever time he wanted and didn't seem to realize that not everyone could sleep in. Plus, you know how I am about people being late *anyway*. It would take me another hour and a half to stop bitching about it.

But once we got all that out of the way, we had a great time. We would just walk all around the city, through Soho, the Village—actually I think we walked every inch of Manhattan, getting coffee or something to eat, buying whatever little *tchotchkes* (also known as crappy little trinkets that are worth nothing and collect dust in a drawer until you sell them at a yard sale) caught our eye. This one guy loved us. Joe bought so much stuff from him, I think he kept the store in business. But mostly we would just lose ourselves in the hustle and bustle and talk, talk, talk. He was going through a lot of stuff, and my personal life was a disaster. But we found something in each other that seemed to make all that other stuff go away, at least while we were together.

In New York, you're anonymous. It's not like being in a small town, where everyone knows your business. You can escape and reinvent yourself. On the other hand, you can escape everything *but* yourself.

Joe and I also used to go to The Duplex—this famous gay bar on the corner of West Fourth Street and Seventh Avenue—and play pool. I was invisible, of course, but Joe got hit on left and right. He was always so cool about it, it was never awkward. He just seemed to fit in everywhere.

I was still really guarded, but I realized that although my relationship with Joe was officially a friendship, it felt like a courtship too. I knew Joe thought of it that way. He wore his heart on his sleeve from day one. And he was constantly asking me, "Do you like me? Do you like me?" I wanted to say, "What is this, the third grade? If I didn't like you, I wouldn't be playing with you every day at recess, would I?" But he didn't look like I thought my Prince Charming was supposed to, and that threw me. I liked him, sure, but did I *like* him, like him?

From the very beginning, Joe was different from the other guys I'd been with. In every way. He broadened my world, and not in the you-gotta-try-this-new-shot kind of way that the guidos down the shore did, or even the let-me-show-you-how-the-country-club-set-lives way like a lot of guys in the city did. No, Joe changed my life in a very profound, even spiritual way. He made me see the world through his eyes and, as anyone who knows my husband would tell you, that is a true privilege.

Joe always helped people, because that is a big part of who Joe is. When people talk about philanthropists, they're usually referring to people who are wealthy enough to give to those in need without overextending themselves. And while I think it's great whenever and however someone chooses to help another person, I also know that Joe has always gone out of his way to be a positive force in people's lives regardless of his own circumstances. This includes giving a dollar to someone who needs it even when he didn't have two nickels to rub together.

I didn't know that about Joe in the beginning. When we first started hanging out, it was really all about the music. Joe has always loved all different kinds of music. My idea of being well-rounded was knowing the top ten on Z100. Joe took me to the Blue Note and other jazz clubs around the city. Then he started giving me his own music to listen to, and that was really incredible. I had never known anyone who wrote their own songs before, and to tell you the truth, at first I didn't know what to expect. I mean, what would I say if I didn't get it? Or, worse, if his music just sucked?

I figured my best strategy was to bring my Walkman on the subway and listen to one of his tapes on the way to work where he couldn't see my reaction. I was so blown away by his lyrics—because they're poetry, really—that I missed my subway stop more than once. I'd realize it a few minutes later, jump up, yell "sonofabitch" or some other choice word, and grab a train in the other direction. One time I ended up in Brooklyn! And for *that* to happen, you know I was impressed.

But we didn't always stay in the city. On the weekends we'd take little road trips. Jump on I-95, the Jersey Turnpike, Garden State—whatever. We used to go to this place in Ocean Grove a lot. There was a shop where they sold little handmade dolls. Joe and his *tchotchkes* again. I can't tell you how many dolls I have from that place. Then I started visiting him in the studio, which to me, sounded so official.

Joe really was—*is*—an amazing musician. Sometimes when he recorded in the studio, I'd go hang out and listen. For some reason, he'd be surrounded by these supermodels—freakishly tall and annoyingly gorgeous. I don't know if there's some kind of ultrasonic dog whistle or something that attracts them, or how that happened. And there I was, all five feet of me. I also went along when he hung out with all these important people in the industry—singers, songwriters, you name it. It was all really cool and really weird at the same time. I mean, who *was* this guy? And what was *I* doing with him?

I'm not sure when exactly, but eventually it dawned on me that this guy was one in a million. Our relationship changed when I finally realized that some of the best gifts in life do not come in a perfect package. And when I say "perfect," what I really mean is according to our preconceived notions of what things are supposed to look like. Once that sunk in, everything changed. I finally started to get it through my head that I was exactly where I was meant to be: hanging out with Joe, missing my stop on the subway, and buying little dolls in Ocean Grove. But that, as I was soon to find out, was only the tip of a very exciting and very unexpected iceberg.

# 21

# A Different Slice of "Pizza"

Maybe some people cross a clearly drawn line into coupledom, but it wasn't really like that with Joe and me. When I look back, the only real line I see is between Before I Met Joe and Everything Since I Met Joe.

Have you ever read any Danielle Steel novels? Ever since I was a kid, I had pictured myself as a character in one of those novels. I guess it's kind of like my love affairs with napping and Gopher. All about the escape. Of course as I got older, I figured that while growing up in Jersey prepares you for the real world, Danielle Steel certainly does not. Life is not a romance novel, after all. At least not all the time.

Once I finally got it, we had moments worthy of Danielle Steel. There were times when I felt like a heroine in one of her books, being "whisked off" to places or finding myself doing things I never imagined.

I started to see that Joe's world was much larger than I had originally thought, and it was very different from mine. Music was only part of it. He had a whole other career in pharmaceuticals, real and legal pharmaceuticals, and a lot of his business was in Europe. He was always flying back and forth for different trade shows and other events, and he started asking me either to go with him or to meet him wherever he happened to be at the time.

In my job, sure, I dealt with people from all over the world, but they always came to me. My travel allowance was more subway tokens and cab fares than transatlantic travel. Up until then, my travel experience mostly involved those flights out to Ohio, with stops in Columbus or Cincinnati, and a few family summer trips via jam-packed van or station wagon to Florida, California, and Vegas.

Not that those weren't great vacations. My sisters and I froze in the Colorado River and roasted in Las Vegas. Some older girl bullied me in San Francisco, and I got in trouble for it, of course. While we were driving down to Florida, we heard the story of a girl who had been eaten by an alligator. All they found was her finger, with the nail still painted. That pretty much set the mood for that trip. Oh, and of course there the long drives through Midwestern cornfields to get to college. That's what I knew. Now Joe was telling me to meet him in Paris, or Geneva, or Venice, and I found myself boarding the Concorde!

It was exciting, but honestly, pretty friggin' intimidating at first. The plane looked like a cross between a rocket ship and a bird with its beak out of joint. And speaking as someone who's not quite sure people were meant to fly, I wasn't exactly comforted by the fact that it went twice as fast as any other plane. I was trapped on an angry bird that would either get me to France *really quickly* or would take a nosedive into the Atlantic.

Not to mention that each flight was a star-studded affair. Which, of course, was exciting, but let me tell you, when you've lived your whole life as a regular person, it's really weird to all of a sudden be surrounded by famous people—people I had only seen on TV, in the movies, and on the occasional cover of *The National Enquirer*.

The first time I took the Concorde, I was headed to Paris. I looked around the plane, hoping against hope that Gopher might be there. Perhaps he had gotten work on a French cruise line and was on his way to report for duty. Maybe he'd be wearing his white uniform and waiting to hand me a mai tai before introducing me to Jerry Stiller and Anne Meara. He wasn't there, of course, but Don King was. The first thing I noticed was his hair (which, believe it or not, is even more outrageous in person);

the second was that he's a pretty big man and the Concorde's seats were really narrow. He managed to squeeze himself in, though. I know because I watched him. I was about to ask him whether Mike Tyson's voice is really that high when I was distracted by Isabella Rossellini. She was there with her kid, and somehow I wound up playing nanny for the entire flight. Because that's what you'd do for *any* stranger on a plane, right?

Celebrities were everywhere—not only on the Concorde—and I have to admit I was star struck. I almost passed out when Joe got into a conversation with Billy Joel at Villa d'Este in Italy. Unfortunately I was also a bit of an idiot. Our boat driver told me he was friends with George Clooney and it was too bad George wasn't in town, implying that he could have arranged an introduction. I completely believed him and felt like an ass when Joe told me the guy was just after a big tip.

That first trip to France was the biggest eye-opener. I went to see Joe's office in Paris, and it was even more shocking to me than when I had visited him at the music studio in Jersey. I mean, this guy had a whole other existence as a businessman, with suits and a corporate card and enough knowledge about the pharmaceutical industry to fill an encyclopedia. And he treated me like the center of this crazy little universe. There we were, sipping drinks at the Plaza Athénée, looking out over the Avenue Montaigne and talking about what it would be like to have two daughters. I was completely lost in the moment, yet there was a part of me standing back and saying, "Are you friggin' kidding me? There is no way this is real." I expected to wake up any moment with my lips pressed against the television screen.

Another time I flew to Venice to meet Joe for a trade show. I boarded the Concorde, excited to see whatever celebrities were there that day. Instead I wound up sitting next to some random, non-famous woman. *Oh well*, I thought. Then I looked down and saw that she had the largest diamond ring I had ever seen sitting quite comfortably on her finger. She probably thought I was nuts when I asked her if I could try it on, but she just smiled, took the ring off, and handed it to me. I must say, it looked much better on me than it did on her, but since it's hard to make off with a diamond ring at sixty-thousand feet, I eventually had to give it back. When I got off the plane I realized I didn't even have enough money for a taxi to the hotel . . . a reminder that this wasn't really my world.

Luckily, Joe did more in Europe than just go to business meetings.

When I found out that there a masquerade ball that was part of a trade show, I had no idea what it would be like. I was half expecting a cheesy costume party where people dress up as hookers and ex-presidents, but it was unlike anything I'd ever read about in a romance novel or seen on *The Love Boat*. More like *Fantasy Island*. The men were in tuxedos and the women in stunning couture, with amazing, artistic masks. The ball wasn't in some local dive bar or even a hotel; it *certainly* wasn't the Pacific Princess. It was an actual castle where the chandeliers were lit with real candles. As I looked around the room, I could not believe this world even existed, let alone that I was in it. I stared at Joe, who looked like a million bucks in his tux, and tried to wrap my head around the fact that this was the guy who had pulled up next to Elissa's house in a wife beater, white high-top sneakers, and enough gold to choke Mr. T.

This trip was also the beginning of a time-honored tradition in our relationship—one I like to call "I have a whim that winds up costing Joe large sums of money." One night in Venice, we went into a store and met these artists who worked with Murano glass. Murano is a tiny island off the coast of Venice, and its citizens have been creating these gorgeous, multicolored glass vases and other items since something like the ninth century. Of course I didn't know any of this when, after a few too many cocktails, I told these people that Joe and I would like to buy their wares and become their agents. I also didn't know that these wares were not just the few pieces they had with them, but a castle-sized warehouse of others as well. In any event, Joe and I wound up buying their entire inventory. We got a bunch of it placed on consignment in stores all over northern New Jersey. The artists were so thrilled, they pledged their undying devotion to their new drunk American friends. They even came to visit us years later, when they were in New York on business. It was their first time in the United States, and we took them to the Blue Note, which was fitting since that's where this all began. To this day, we don't know whether we made money, lost money, or broke even on the deal. But I think Murano has a holiday named after us.

On these trips, I started meeting some of Joe's friends and business associates, and we spent a lot of time hanging out in their homes, which were nothing like my childhood home, or on their boats, which were a far cry from my father's old rowboat. These were what they thought of as very casual get-togethers: talking, drinking, eating, that kind of thing.

And people with vast amounts of money do things very differently. It's not always better, though, as I found out.

One day we were on this couple's yacht, and everything was great, but there was something missing. Finally we realized what it was: music! Back home, we would have turned on the Bose and problem solved, but not here, not in this world. We had seen oompah bands on the street—the ones with the trumpets and accordions that play polka music. For some reason, it seemed like a great idea to have them play on the boat while we had dinner! So we hired the next band we saw. They were thrilled when we asked them; they weren't so happy when they were lugging the four-hundred-pound accordion onto the boat. Who knew these people had so much equipment?

After all the set-up, they started to play, and for the first few minutes I was like, okay, this is cool. Sort of. Five minutes in we all looked at each other and said, "Wow—this music really sucks." But we had to let them play for a while—they had gone to so much effort. We eventually thanked them and sent them on their way. It's so much easier to change the station or just turn the music off.

Another time Joe called and asked if I wanted to "come over for dinner" on Saturday night. Silly me, I was thinking he meant at his house in Jersey. After all, he'd said it so casually that for a minute I'd thought I had my dates screwed up. "But aren't you in Switzerland this weekend?"

"Yup."

And that was how I wound up flying to Switzerland . . . for one amazing meal. Joe was staying at the Beau Rivage in Geneva, which is only one of the most incredible resorts in the world. Too bad I really didn't get to see it. I flew in at night, exhausted, jetlagged, and starving. I had been looking forward to seeing Switzerland, but in the dark it's really no different from any other place. I know I went over a bridge, but for all I knew (or cared) at that point, it could have been the Goethals Bridge in Jersey.

After dinner I was ready to crash. The problem was, there was an oompah band—unfortunately they're all over the place in Europe—playing outside our room. It kept us up all night, and I flew back home the next day practically comatose and wondering how I was going to make it through the week at work. To make matters worse, it took about a month to get the sound of trumpets and accordions out of my head. I think it was friggin' karma—payment for making that poor oompah band in Venice lug their stuff on and off the boat.

To this day, I cringe whenever I hear polka music.

# 22

# The "Mane" Attraction

———

These trips with Joe opened my eyes to a completely different world. A world that not even the rich fantasy life of my childhood could have prepared me for. Between the five-star hotels, the grand events, and the shopping trips, I started to learn about quality—not something I had ever really thought about. I mean, I was doing really well at my job back in New York, but to me, "really well" meant not sharing a bathroom with seven other people or wearing my sisters' hand-me-downs. What Joe introduced me to was as foreign to me as my hygiene lessons were to the international computer programmers who thought it was okay not to wash their clothes and fart at will. Needless to say, there was a bit of culture shock—and sticker shock—involved.

It was on one of these trips that I bought my very first designer bag, which, as I found out, is a rite of passage in certain circles. Each of the cities I visited in Europe—Venice, Paris, Geneva—was amazing and unique. But they also had one very important thing in common: every step I took landed me in front of another fabulous boutique. One of these steps landed me in front of a Salvatore Ferragamo store, and Joe and I went in. I don't know what happened to me when I was in there, but it was like I fell under some sort of spell. The smell of the leather, the rich fabrics, and the chic salesgirls all conspired against me. And when we walked out, I was carrying a bag I had paid a whopping $640 for. I literally felt sick to my stomach. Especially since I had no friggin' clue what I had actually paid after the exchange rate (remember, my boss had to lecture me about how to figure out a tip, and that had been in New York, using American money).

Joe was completely at ease with all this luxury; it was simply another part of the life he had built for himself. When we were in Paris, I remember watching him as he joked around with yet another celebrity or billionaire, and I thought, *Is this the same guy from the Jersey shore?* It didn't seem possible, but it had to be him. No other man on Avenue Montaigne had hair that long.

Like most things in life, not everything in the new world was as good as it looked. Shoes, for example: I was shopping in Venice with Lisa (a dear friend and the wife of Joe's business partner, Jean Luc). The shoes were hot, and like a little devil on my shoulder, Lisa said I *had* to buy them. I agreed. But that fat price tag should have come with a warning: Treacherous When Raining. I slipped and slid all the way back to the hotel like Bambi learning to walk. Lisa, when she wasn't hysterically laughing, held on to my arm; when *I* wasn't hysterically laughing, I was trying not to fall on my ass.

It wasn't just the stuff—the bags and the shoes. It was also the people. When Joe and I were staying in a castle in Italy, one part of me was still like, "Wow, castle!" while the other part of me was saying, "Yeah, that's incredible, but what is this I hear about Sting being the next-door neighbor?" Then, I found myself seated next to him at the Italian Movie Awards and, although I wanted desperately to speak to him, I just sat there, frozen.

And speaking of frozen, so was the castle. I guess I should have remembered there was no central heating during the Middle Ages. It wasn't just cold, it was deep-in-your-bones, there-are-not-enough-blankets-in-the-world cold. Joe and I got out of bed in the middle of the night and put on every piece of clothing in our suitcases just so we could go to sleep. Fortunately Joe has always been a heavy packer; he still always gets pulled out of the line at the airport and is asked to check his extra carry-ons. While I've been annoyed by this many times since that trip (mostly because I pride myself on being a highly efficient packer who only takes the necessities), on that night in Italy I was extremely grateful. Thanks to Joe, we had a month's worth of sport jackets, sweaters, jeans, shorts, and socks to put on, and that was how we avoided frostbite in that beautiful, but seriously uncomfortable, Italian castle.

Like staying in castles, the world of private jets and charter planes sounds so luxurious, but it isn't always. One time, on our way to St. Thomas to meet Marco, Joe's business partner, we took a "puddle jumper" that looked more like you might imagine a mosquito to look like if it grew to four thousand times its size and was made of tin. It sounded like one and flew like one. When we finally landed, I was so relieved we were alive and that I had managed not to lose my lunch. But Marco was an interesting guy and one of the few people who openly supported my relationship with Joe. (Some people have a problem with it because of our age difference.)

The tin mosquito wasn't the worst plane I've been on. We took a private plane over to St. Bart's from Puerto Rico. "Private plane" sounds nice, right? Except that this one was as old as dirt. So old that the pilot (who looked like he was barely out of diapers) was complaining about it. If that's not scary enough, when you fly to St. Bart's you have to fly through an opening between two cliffs. If you miss it, you're dead. I figured this out by looking out the window at the many crosses to memorialize the victims. Oh, and if you overshoot the runway, you end up on the beach or in the ocean. Also dead. And not you-drown-for-a-minute-then-are-saved-by-good-Samaritans dead.

As soon as we landed, the first order of business was to make arrangements for a real plane to get us home. The second order of business was to pick up the Jeep we were renting for the week and hope it wasn't also a death trap. Third order of business: check in at the hotel, the Isle de France, and try to ignore the stares from just about everyone that said, "Oh, you can't *possibly* be staying here." Just because we looked like we'd just left a Warrant concert meant we didn't belong?

The next day on the beach, it was the same thing. Except the stares came from topless Europeans with bodies that would have made Gisele Bündchen jealous. I was pretty sure that they were all trying to figure out what rock band Joe was with. I wanted to turn to them and say, "PS the hair is real."

Being from New Jersey, I was sure I was a trendsetter in fashion. I didn't see anyone else dressed like I was, with neon pink nails and eye-numbing color combinations, but I figured I was ahead of the curve. In Jersey, we don't stray from what is shown in the mall season to season. We buy fad clothes, not the staple pieces. As I traveled with Joe, I started to learn the difference, and, little by little, figured that, actually, the opposite was true.

I started to get the idea when we had visited one of Joe's partners, Rino, in Italy. In addition to the banks his family owned, Rino dabbled in art (meaning he had a collection worth millions) and enjoyed a good bottle of wine (meaning he owned a vineyard). He knew people like Ferragamo and the owner of Ruffino wine. In other words, if Florence had a royal family, Rino would be the king. He'd married Renelle, a model from New Orleans, and sometimes I wondered how the blending of those two cultures worked. I imagined them eating catfish Fra Diavolo and listening to operas sung by Blues Traveler.

Renelle and Rino had two young daughters, Anya and Ariella, and although they had American blood running through their veins, they were essentially Italians—wealthy and cultured Italians. Which meant they didn't know what to make of me at all. We were having dinner with them one night and I noticed that seven-year-old Ariella couldn't take her eyes off my hands. Or, rather, my fake, pink nails. Renelle noticed it, too, and finally had to explain to her daughter that it was "what they did" in America. That was when I realized that with my nails and my big hair, I was a caricature. I was That Girl from Jersey they saw only in mafia movies and on reality TV shows. But I digress.

When we got back to the Jeep, it had a flat. No big deal. Everybody was watching us. My father's first call would have been to AAA. But not Joe. Within minutes we had a spare tire on and were ready to go. I could only imagine what people were thinking then: "Howard Stern, fixing his own tire? Bloody Americans!"

When Joe and I had started going out, I'd often had the feeling that we were never alone. It was the strangest thing, like a mysterious presence was following us around. Finally, after getting the millionth stare from a snotty concierge, I figured it out: it was his Hair. It had a personality and life of its own. It tried to mind its own business, but always caused a stir nonetheless. Once, after visiting Joe's office in Paris, we took the bullet train to Geneva to visit Jean Luc and Lisa. And, as always, security pulled him aside, thinking he was either a rocker or a drug dealer. It was his Hair, of course, but they didn't care. They tore apart his luggage, right down to his friggin' deodorant. (Thinking there might be drugs inside, which, of course, there weren't. When they tried to give it back to him, Joe calmly told them to keep it. To his credit, his Hair remained silent.) And where was I during all this? About fifty feet ahead. I learned early on that when we went anywhere with a security checkpoint, I should put as much distance between myself and his Hair as possible if I wanted to get through without a million questions.

Of course it wouldn't be fair to blame his Hair for everything. Like the time we stayed at a private villa in Annecy, France. First it was dinner with Jean Luc and Lisa, then a walk to digest the seven courses (and a fair amount of booze). Joe, who had stayed there several times before, suggested heading to the hotel-casino down the street. He didn't have to say it twice. Joe couldn't care less about gambling, but I love it. I also never miss to a chance to rub elbows with a movie star or two. So basically the Hotel Royal Palace is my Mecca.

There was a man playing in the piano bar, so we sat and watched and had our hundredth drink. And when the guy took a break a few minutes later, Joe asked if he could play. The guy said yes without even knowing if Joe had an ounce of musical ability (I'm thinking it wasn't Joe at all, but his Hair), and it wasn't long before the "American musician" had the entire bar singing and laughing. The owner told us it was an honor and we could come back anytime. All in all, a great night.

Until we stumbled back to our villa and rang the bell at the gates. No answer. No big deal, right? We'll just keep trying. No one answered, and we didn't have cell phones. We also weren't about to climb a thirty-foot fence. (Which, I thought, was funny and a bit ironic. Luxury villas. High security. To keep the riffraff out. Then I remembered his Hair.) We had to walk back to the hotel and ask the people at the front desk to call our villa and have them open the gates. By the time we got back and actually got inside, the sun was coming up. Some people are up all night partying, drinking, and gambling. We try to avoid arrest for breaking and entering.

The next night we were invited to a party with Jean Luc's friends. And not one of them spoke English. But they did all know American songs, so Joe sat and played on the piano once again, and everyone sang in perfect

English. Once the music stopped, that was it—no more conversation. If Joe were a diplomat, the world would be a different place. No one would know what the other was saying, but he'd sing "We Are the World" and everyone would go home happy.

From there, we were off to Cannes to meet Jan, Jean Luc's son. The plan was for Jan to meet Joe and me at our suite at the Ritz-Carlton and take us to the city's most popular nightclub. First we went to the beach, where we got the usual strange stares from topless women and men in Speedos. As usual, I was amazed by their lack of inhibition. *If these people can let it all hang out*, I thought, *why can't I?* At least that was what I thought after a fair amount of wine, which I had needed to drink to deal with the Speedos.

Later that evening and dressed to kill, we headed to the club. Which was indeed packed. And fabulous. The only problem was it was Michael Jackson night. That meant all Michael Jackson. All night. In the United States (at least anywhere in the Tri-State Area), this would have been unacceptable (and down the shore, possibly the start of a riot). In Cannes, it was the party of the year. The place was packed with Europeans ecstatically dancing to "Rock with You," with impressive enthusiasm and interesting interpretations of Jackson's signature moves. I felt like I was in a French version of *Saturday Night Fever* and that any minute Gerard Depardieu would walk in wearing a tight, white suit and start doing the hustle. After a few glasses of wine, Joe and I joined right in. When in Rome . . . or wherever!

I loved the traveling, but sometimes it was nice just to be home. Especially when home was New York City. And especially when we got to entertain our friends in Manhattan rather than getting locked out of villas or frisked by security in Europe. One Valentine's Day, Jean Luc and Lisa happened to be in town, so Joe and I took them to Café des Artistes for a double date.

It's gone now, but for decades Café des Artistes was a fixture on the Upper West Side, famous for both its artwork and its food. That night it was especially packed for Valentine's Day, and between the noise, the paintings, and the steak tartare, I had a pretty good case of sensory overload.

However, I just happened to glance at the next table as the man was handing the woman a Cartier box. I gave Lisa the eye that said, "It is our womanly duty to inspect the contents and possibly make catty remarks about it." The joke was on us, though, because that necklace was gorgeous and obviously worth a mint. I looked at Lisa and mouthed, "Wow." What I wanted to say was, "Lisa, close your mouth before you catch a fly." Her jaw was practically on the table.

Given my surprise at the extravagant gift, it was a bit of a shock (okay, it felt more like a coronary) when a few weeks later, Joe gave me a one-of-a-kind Rolex that completely took my breath away. As I opened the box, Lisa's face flashed through my mind. And speaking of flies, what I would have given to be a fly on the wall when Joe and his Hair walked in to buy the watch. The look on the associate's face. Finger on the panic button. Torn between calling security and asking for his autograph.

I've always told Joe that he's three in one: the man who runs an international company, the guy who combs flea markets, and the musician. He fixes tires in St. Bart's and makes friends with Paul McCartney on a flight to Europe. Paul even sang him a song as they waited for the luggage. Joe always did have good luck on the Concorde, especially since security didn't treat him like a member of Al Qaeda. And he always came home with a story about helping Mariah Carey fill out papers on her first trip to Europe or partying with Eric Clapton. One day we were trolling a flea market in the West Village. I watched, trying to keep a straight face, as the vendors eyed Joe up and down and clucked their teeth with pity. *Poor thing, he can't even afford a haircut.* They gave him a great discount.

# 23

# The Parent Trap

———

It would be nice to be able to say that once Joe and I started really dating, it was all smooth sailing. Not exactly. In fact, it was more like a stormy North Atlantic . . . with icebergs. A Stephen King novel after a lifetime of Danielle Steel. Especially when it came to my family.

To this day, I'm not quite sure what their biggest issue was. I think it might have been the age difference. When I went to Joe's shore house on the day we met, I saw pictures of his sons Joey and Jeffrey. *Okay, so he has kids*, I remember thinking, *but how old* is *this guy?* As I soon found out, Joe has about twenty years on me.

I guess like every other family, mine had an idea of with whom I should settle down. My dad was the mayor of our town, and probably envisioned me with some perfect, golf club-wielding Ken doll–type I could bring to local functions. Someone around my age who had never been married before. Someone who didn't already have kids. Someone who didn't look like they were the lead singer of a rock band. In other words, someone who looked good on paper.

Instead I fell for a forty-something guy with hair down his back, a musician (which for some reason in my parents' minds cancelled out the fact that he also owned a pharmaceutical company), divorced, with two children of his own, plus two foster sons from Nigeria.

They were not at all impressed by all the places he took me. All the jet-setting and fancy places made them trust him *less*, if that was possible. In the grand tradition of the family who brought you wedding boycotts and knife fights, my parents and sisters sort of stayed away from my life. While Joe and I were having the time of our lives, traveling the world and listening to oompah bands, they were back in New Jersey just waiting to deliver the big "we told you so."

I'm glad they finally got over all that.

The best was my father. He'd always been big on giving jewelry to my mom, my sisters, and me, but he was floored when he saw the pieces Joe gave me. Part of me wanted to say, "And this is the guy you wanted me to dump so I could find someone with less hair, no kids, and a set of golf clubs." But the look on Dad's face was enough for me. It was like the Visa commercial: one-of-a-kind Rolex, $300,000; tank of gas to drive to your parents' house in New Jersey, $50; look on your father's face when he's 1,000 percent wrong, priceless.

My grandmother, God rest her soul, supported Joe and me from the beginning. She loved Joe immediately, I think partially because he reminded her of my grandfather, who had passed away when I was in college. I remember that our family and friends used to call Grandpa "crafty" because he was so handy around the house, and Joe is the same way. He knows all about construction and stuff like that, and whenever I brought him by my grandmother's, he would fix things for her. No one could say a bad word about Joe after that. Whatever else might happen, she figured, I would never have to hang a picture frame or caulk a leaky tub again.

"I don't know what's wrong with your mother," she'd say whenever my family's attitude toward Joe came up. "I don't know why any of them are like this. It's your life—they should just accept it."

Even Anthony felt "a little strange" about Joe and me together. "And, let's face it," he told me, "he looked like a rocker. You know what I mean, Lauren. With the hair and the hat . . . c'mon."

Back when I lived in the West Village, Anthony was home from college in Virginia. He drove to Jersey with some friends and the girl he was dating at the time and he came to see me in the city. I was pretty serious with Joe by then. The three of us wound up eating at an Italian place that was one of Joe's favorites, and the food was delicious. They also used to sing "Happy Birthday" all the time, and that night, thank God, there were at least three birthdays.

Usually it would be really annoying to have to keep listening to "Happy Birthday" over and over again, but in this situation, it was a relief. It gave me something to concentrate on besides Anthony staring at Joe as if he were deciding whether to kill him or ask him to pass the rolls. Anthony had always been very protective of me, so I know he was going to make sure this long-haired rocker guy was worthy of me. He wanted to see for himself whether my family was justified in shunning him or was just acting nuts, which he knew full well they were capable of being. After dinner, Anthony admitted, "He seemed like a very normal guy and nice. It wasn't like he *said* anything strange. He just *looked* strange."

To be fair to my skeptical family, Joe wasn't my usual type, except that he was older. I have to admit that I've always had a bit of a caretaker thing with men (or at least that's what my therapist told me). My older brother took such good care of me when I was little, I guess he set the bar. This appreciation for older men continued throughout my childhood— my first loves were all older than I was: Gopher, of course, and the Fonz and John Travolta in *Grease*.

When I started dating real people instead of kissing the television screen, it was always with guys a few years older than me. If I was a freshman in high school, my boyfriend was a junior. When I was a freshman in college, I dated someone who was a senior, and when I was a junior, I kicked it up to a guy seven years older. When I met Joe, I knew he was older, but he didn't look *that* much older—maybe it was the Hair. I didn't find out he was two decades older than me for a long time, and by the time I found out, I was already hooked.

I wasn't all that shocked by their reactions. Michelle was the only one who was there for me. She didn't need explanations about why I was with Joe, and I didn't offer any (mostly 'cause I didn't know what was going on myself). I just told her I had "met someone" and she was going to come with us to a Phil Collins concert (and before you say anything about that, remember this was the nineties). Private room and a limo. Michelle had a great time at that concert. Like Anthony, she noticed that Joe was not the kind of guy I usually went for. And of course she also noticed his "different" rocker look. But she saw it like my grandmother did: as long as I was happy, it was all good. Happiness—what a novel friggin' idea!

Michelle has known me my whole life, inside and out. So from the minute she saw Joe and me together, she knew this was a completely different ballgame. She told me that she knew, by the way I was looking at him, that I thought he was "the one." And that was good enough for her.

# 24

# A Feverish Proposal

—

I've set the bar pretty high with the dating stories about castles and jetting off to Europe for dinner, so you'd expect the proposal to be a fairy tale—Joe dressed in tux and tails, getting down on one knee in a villa in the south of France. Well, south, kind of. France, no.

I had told Joe about my prayer on the beach that morning just a few minutes before he went roaring by in his Ferrari. So—and this is *so* Joe—when he was ready to propose, he thought it only fitting to take me back to that spot. He also decided to ask me on my birthday, which was incredibly sweet. Except that my birthday is in December, or, as we like to call it in the northeastern United States, the dead of friggin' winter. Bitter cold and icy winds, which you can easily multiply by ten if you're down the shore. Oh, and did I mention I had the flu? Chills, fever, aches, and pain. The works. As we traipsed through the frozen sand, I felt so lousy I thought I might have been having another near-death experience (or at least I almost wished for one). Despite having a bottle of champagne (that I couldn't drink because I was so sick), Joe still pretended I didn't know why we were there. I went along with the charade, thinking he'd *better* be proposing, because if he wasn't, I was going to kill him.

So it was there, shouting to be heard over roaring waves, howling gales, and my chattering teeth, that Joe asked me to be his wife. He told me how much he loved me and that although he was worried about how his sons would accept this, he wanted more than anything for us to be married. Basically, in the end, the proposal was like everything else about our relationship: from the outside it seemed a little messy, but in reality it was magic.

After I said yes—as quickly as possible, so we could get the hell off the beach and under a heated blanket—I called my mother. By that time, my parents had decided to give up their dream of me marrying Jersey's answer to Prince Charles and accept the fact that I would be spending my life with Joe. Which was good timing, because I was counting on my mother's florist shop to supply the flowers for the wedding.

"I have some news, Ma. Joe asked me to marry him."

There was silence on the other end, and for a moment I thought we had been disconnected. Or could my mother finally have been rendered speechless?

No such luck.

"Did you hear what I said? Joe proposed and I said yes. Ma? You there?"

"Of course I'm here." Pause. "So tell me, how big is the ring?"

# 25

# From Danielle Steel to *Lord of the Flies*

My wedding, again, was not in a villa in the south of France. I was not a bridezilla, and there was no paparazzi helicoptering over an exclusive island. It was a bit . . . low-maintenance, actually.

Joe and I got married about seven months after the proposal. We threw the wedding together, maybe because from the beginning nothing went according to plan anyway. We had to change churches and redo the invitations two weeks before the wedding. Most people would have lost their shit if this had happened, but very early on I had decided that nothing was going to stress me out on the day I married Joe.

It almost got to be a running joke. Calling the band, the hall, or whatever and asking about their dates of availability, prices, and so on. And us saying, "That's fine, that's fine," to everything. In the end, though, it lived up to all my childhood fantasies. Joe booked the Stony Hill Inn in Hackensack, a place that usually holds two weddings at a time and has an enormous restaurant to boot. They had never rented out the entire place before, but Joe worked his magic. As with my prayer that had brought us together and Joe's marriage proposal, the beach took center stage, with five-foot-high arrangements of sand and shells on each table. We had the usual wedding-day issues, of course—some European guests unexpectedly brought their kids and we hadn't factored them into the seating arrangement; it was an August day so hot we felt like we were in Calcutta instead of New Jersey—but all in all, it was great.

Believe it or not, I actually wore the same dress I was supposed to wear to my wedding to Mr. Melt. I mean, after all, it was a beautiful little princess dress. And as my mother said, "You already paid for it. Why not?" Always the pragmatist. Which was fine. I took that moment to remind my mother we would, in fact, be using her florist shop for the flowers. My parents even insisted on giving us money to pay for the wedding, which I thought was wonderful.

While my dress became dress-up fare for my daughter (and, okay, me too, sometimes) and has gone missing in one of our many moves, I have so many wonderful pictures of the wedding itself—several shots of Joe and me, arms locked, sipping beer from cans. We had that Heather Locklear–rocker vibe going on. Unfortunately there are no pictures of my father-in-law going around to collect the cards from each and every gift, thinking there was money in them and wanting to keep them safe. If we did have those pictures, we might actually know who gave us what. (Writing out the thank-you cards was fun: "Dear Aunt So-and-So, I really appreciate that beautiful . . . uh . . . yeah.")

We both look really happy in those photos, and we were. We weren't nervous, no cold feet. I was 100 percent sure this was right.

That feeling lasted until we arrived at Anguilla for the honeymoon. Also known as The Week from Hell. Even though I was sick as a dog for the marriage proposal and wished I could have that to do over again, and there were so many curve balls thrown at the wedding, it was the honeymoon that really took the cake.

For most of the year, this place might be very lovely. It certainly had sounded that way when we'd booked it. The only problem was the person on the other end had neglected to tell us that the week we were considering was fly-mating season. Which lasted just one week. Out of the whole year. This means that in addition to Joe, me, and some other unlucky couples, millions of flies were just hanging out, waiting to get it on. There were swarms of them everywhere: by the pool, at the bar . . . Everywhere we went, we felt like we were feeling our way through a thick, black cloud. There was no escape, so we chose to cut our honeymoon short and go back to the good, old Jersey Shore.

# 26

# Boxers, Babies, and the Snapple Facts of Life

———

Joe and I wanted to have kids right away. But this proved to be more of a challenge than I'd anticipated. Which is rather funny, when you think about it. I had, like so many women, spent a good portion of my early childbearing years trying to avoid pregnancy (using everything from abstinence to condoms to good old-fashioned prayers—"Please, God, I promise never to do 'it' again—just don't let me be pregnant"); in high school and college it felt like as much of a goal as making the cheerleading team or passing algebra. Then suddenly, when I wanted kids, it turned out not to be so easy. It's like the entire world is operating in reverse: you schedule unprotected sex and cry when you get your period on time.

Men have their crosses to bear as well. Joe had to start wearing boxers and completely rearrange his social calendar. In fact, it became a running joke among his friends. One of the guys would ask him, "So, Joe, what are you doing tonight?" And his answer would be, "Probably the same thing as last night." And not with the kind of enthusiasm you might hope for, as the blushing bride and future mother of his children.

Naturally, because we weren't getting pregnant, everyone around us was. It seemed like everyone at work was waddling around and eating for two, and that was just the men. I felt like there was this giant to-do list, and Joe and I were falling behind schedule. I bought him looser boxers and told him not to make any plans until further notice.

When I finally did conceive, I knew right away. Well, I didn't *know*, but I had a strong feeling. I felt different. Then again, I knew it could just have been wishful thinking. Or indigestion from the chicken parmigiana I had eaten the night before. I ran to CVS and down the women's aisle. There, between the tampons and the incontinence products, were eight gazillion types of pregnancy tests. After reading the boxes of about half of them, I caught hold of myself. It didn't matter which test I bought—either I was pregnant or I wasn't. I grabbed one and headed for the register. The line was so long, I thought that if I *was* pregnant, I might actually give birth before I got a chance to pay. I passed the time on line contemplating the headlines for that one.

"Do you have a ladies' room I can use?" I asked the cashier—a girl around seventeen years old—when it was finally my turn. She looked at me, then down at the test, then back at me. I could almost see the different scenarios running through her mind. How I was going to pee on the test in the store. Why I had to find out so quickly. I imagined her telling her friends later about the cautionary tale in her line that day. I found this pretty funny. But hey, if it helped her pass the time, what did I care? As long as she didn't announce it on the PA system.

She pointed to a far corner of the store. I paused for a moment because she looked like she was dying to ask me a question, but then she glanced at the customers piled up behind me and sighed. I thanked her and moved swiftly down the nearest aisle, glad I'd had that big cup of coffee before leaving the house.

Peeing on the stick was fairly easy (although it would have been easier at home, where I wasn't trying to avoid touching anything). The hard part was waiting the three minutes for the results. Three minutes for my life to completely and irrevocably change. Possibly. When I saw the test was positive, I was so happy I wanted to scream out loud. I held it in for the cashier's sake, figuring she'd had enough excitement for one day.

Instead I walked back to an aisle I had passed before. An aisle of *tchotchkes*. There were little figurines of babies. I picked up a little boy and a little girl, thinking it was the perfect way to give Joe the news. I went to another cashier's line to pay for them.

I've always heard you're not to supposed to tell anyone until after three months, when you're out of the so-called "danger zone" of the first trimester. But I had never paid much attention to how you're supposed to do things, and I wasn't about to start now. I told everyone I was pregnant right away.

The only thing better than the positive pee test was finding out the baby was a girl. Although the way I found out pretty much sucked. I was about three months along when I started having really severe back pain. Which, when coupled with pregnancy, basically feels like God is punishing you. I don't usually think like that, but it's hard to be upbeat when you're tired and nauseated, and you have the added bonus of feeling like someone is stabbing you in the back with an ice pick. Just when I was about to go to confession, it hit me: this wasn't karma, it was the return of my old friend, the kidney stone. Instead of going to church, I made a beeline for my urologist's office (and said a few Hail Marys just to be on the safe side). I had passed a million of these stones before (actually, it was about twenty, but if you've ever passed one you know it's better not to argue with me), so I knew the drill: ultrasound followed by recommended dietary restrictions and finally waiting for the little bugger to pass.

So there I was, in my hospital gown, flinching as the tech applied jelly that's always freezing no matter what the season. She would wave the magic wand, look at the screen, and confirm the diagnosis. Except that she confirmed a lot more than that. Who knew they'd tell me the sex of the baby? When they told me it was a girl, I was so happy I almost forgot about the pain. Almost. The women in the office were almost as excited as I was (which made sense, considering it was a urologist's office and it was probably a nice change from what they usually discovered).

I got dressed and headed for the doctor's office for the usual "are you eating too much cheese?" conversation. He walked in, smiling, my chart in hand. "Looks like we gave you some good news today."

"Absolutely," I said, popping open a Snapple.

He pointed to the bottle. "Do you drink a lot of that?"

"Not too much. Maybe three or four a day."

The smile disappeared. "Well, here's the bad news. You're going to have to cut down. A lot."

He proceeded to tell me that iced tea has an ingredient that has been linked with kidney stones, which I refused to believe, because how could something "made from the best stuff on earth" cause so much agony? Besides, I'd learned a lot of stuff from reading the Snapple "Real Facts" on the insides of the caps. Stuff that's really important to everyday life, like "India has a bill of rights for cows," or "mosquitoes are attracted to people who have just eaten bananas." But I was later told by a doctor friend that kidney stones skyrocketed when Snapple and other iced teas came on the market, which might have explained my twenty.

This doctor then told me to limit myself to either one Snapple or one coffee a day. I thought about how tired I had been feeling and how much worse it was going to be without a steady caffeine supply. Maybe I *should* have gone to confession.

In the meantime, I followed his advice. I saved my caffeine allowance for the time of day that's toughest for any New Yorker, pregnant or not: the morning commute on the subway. For those of you not familiar with this phenomenon, picture thousands of zombies who are pissed they have to get up early and ride this moving Petri dish of disease to work, fighting for the few seats that aren't taken or covered with some unknown substance. Basically it's *The Walking Dead* with iPods. Caffeine is *definitely* required.

Plus the smell of the subway, which ranges in any given minute from urine to chocolate cake to Old Spice, is enough to make anyone barf. So it's nice to have a hot cup of coffee or a peach-flavored tea to hold under your nose.

As if that weren't enough, my daughter never stopped moving around—the entire pregnancy. The worst was when I turned the car radio on. It was like I was back in that club in Cannes—another bad version of *Saturday Night Fever*. Except this time I couldn't escape with a few glasses of wine. I was carrying the most active baby in history, and to this day I wonder if it was the caffeine. I guess I'll never know because Snapple doesn't have a Real Fact for that one.

Kidney stone aside, Joe and I were both thrilled. We picked out little-girl clothes and little-girl furniture. We mentally planned her first birthday party. My thoughts even ran to a sweet sixteen and prom and, one day, even a wedding. In between there would be facials, nail appointments, and shopping for school clothes.

The joy over the child's gender lasted for the next six months, in fact right up until the moment labor began. After that, I really didn't care whether it was a boy or a girl because I knew without a doubt that *it* was trying to kill me.

It was a Friday morning early in December. When the contractions started, my first thought was, *This kid's early!* My second thought was, *I can't believe I'm even* having *a kid*, and my third thought was, *Shit, I'm supposed to go to Joe's company Christmas party tonight.*

Joe was still sleeping, and I waited until the contractions were five minutes apart to tell him it was time to go to the hospital. I didn't know whether it was because he already had kids or simply because he's a man, but when I shook him awake, in pain and more than a little nervous, he sat up, rubbed his eyes, and said, "Mind if I take a quick shower before we head over there?" Totally calm.

That was the first time I considered murdering him. And his Hair, which I knew would take forever to dry.

When we finally left the house, I noticed it was a full moon. Which made sense. It took all my strength not to howl at it because the pain was getting even more intense. I took this as a sign that it was almost over (or at least I told myself that when I wasn't panting). I would go in, slip into an unflattering gown, and pop her out. But of course that wasn't the way it went down. First of all, the hospital was packed. Apparently, it always is when there's a full moon. Like we're a nation of secret werewolves or something. Second, when I slipped into the gown and put my feet in the stirrups, I was told that despite feeling like my insides were being ripped apart, I wasn't dilated at all. Not even a centimeter. And third, the place was under construction and a lot of the rooms were closed off. *No room at the inn, Mrs. Pizza.* So, they said, I might as well go home and walk.

*Walk?* I could barely friggin' stand. Not to mention that I was already pissed that I had bought a fancy dress (not an easy thing when you're nine months pregnant—"Uh, I'll take that muumuu over there, please . . . in *black*") for a Christmas party I would not be attending.

The night before, I had gone to Garden State Plaza to finish my Christmas shopping. Which was a blast. Crowded. Overheated. Waddling from store to store with bags in both arms and a basketball in my belly. A basketball that bounced around to every beat of "Jingle Bell Rock" or "Santa Claus Is Coming to Town."

After leaving the mall, I headed to Chili's to have dinner with my two sisters and their kids, aged two, three, and five. So, collectively, ten years of unrestrained energy. They tore through the place like a three-midget wrecking crew. By the end of our meal, everyone in the place knew their names. I blame them for sending me into labor. My daughter, little gymnast that she was, couldn't wait another day to join her cousins.

When the doctor at the hospital told me to go home, I said, "No way." They said, in that case, they'd have to dilate me. I took a moment to weigh my decision. On the one hand, I'd heard being dilated is incredibly painful. On the other hand, my daughter was clearly ready to get out—maybe she didn't want to be a Christmas baby. Plus I already had the shower planned at my house in a few weeks, and since my family has always been superstitious about showers, I figured it was better just to have the baby now and know that everything was okay.

"Fine," I told them, sounding braver than I felt. "Let's go."

I learned that the term *incredibly painful*—at least when it comes to being dilated—is a gross understatement. You know how they ask you to rate your pain on a scale of one to ten, with ten being the worst pain you've ever felt? I've had kidney stones, so I knew ten . . . and believe me, this was like a fifteen. While I lay there writhing in agony, what were my husband and his Hair doing? Walking the halls, which he knew quite well since he was on the board of the hospital, and finding some of his doctor buddies, who he then brought into my room to say hello. Like this would be a great time for me to meet his friends and have a nice chat. I didn't know if it was the pain, the full moon, or simply the fact that he's a man, but it was the second time I wanted to kill him. But the contractions were just the warm-up act. When it was finally time to push, the pain pushed up to a twenty or maybe thirty.

"Why didn't you tell me it was going to be so hard?" I screamed at the nurse. "I brought makeup!"

Just when I thought I would split in two, our daughter, Ariela, made her entrance into the world. The doctor clocked the time at 5:53 p.m., which for some reason irked Joe, who claimed it was 5:52, like our house number. Like I gave a shit.

Later that night, the nurse came in to announce that my aunt and uncle had come to see me. It took all my energy to raise an eyebrow at her, wondering which aunt and uncle had bothered to visit.

My mom hadn't even showed up, but my electrician and his wife came. We were putting an addition on the house, so he was there all the time . . . my mom was probably playing bridge or something.

Anyway, later on Joe says, "Hon, you mind if I stop by the party?" And around nine o'clock, wearing his baby bracelet, he went to celebrate. I didn't know whether it was the full moon, or because he was a man, or because I was thrilled about my daughter being born, but I couldn't have cared less. I was still annoyed about the dress, though.

I had almost convinced myself that the pain was worth it, when the nurse came in and told me that all the babies in the nursery were sleeping. Except mine. That was when I knew I was screwed.

We named her Ariela, a name we had fallen in love with when we met Joe's partner in Florence, Rino, who had a daughter called Ariella—only with two l's. The thing is, we disagreed on the spelling. Joe swore up and down that there was one l; I said that Rino and every other Italian would spell it with two. After much debate, I gave in, figuring he might know better than I did, given that Rino was his business partner.

It's always nice to be proven right, no matter how it happens. Especially when it comes in the form of several cases of wine that arrived from Rino's vineyard—each bottle, along with the card, labeled Arie*ll*a.

I looked at my husband. "What do you say now, genius?"

We brought Ariela home in the middle of a snowstorm (also known as I Had No Clue What the Hell I Was in for Day; we usually have a snowstorm around her birthday to commemorate). Because, like all new mothers, I had no idea what I was getting into. If we did, women would never have children, and the human race would cease to exist. Ariela looked like a perfectly normal human baby, but she acted more like an alien species—at least it seemed that way to me at the time. Unlike other babies, she didn't seem to require food or rest. She didn't think anyone else needed them either. How many days can *you* go without sleep? Let's just say you don't want to find out. Michelle thought I was nuts when I packed the baby up in the car and drove around with her, sometimes for over an hour, just so she would fall asleep. Nuts, no. Desperate, yes. Michelle learned this lesson the hard way after she had a baby who was exactly the same.

After Ariela's birth, I was falling on my face, and not just in an I'm-so-tired-I-can't-even-stay-up-for-the-eleven-o'clock-news type of way. It was more like an I-don't-know-the-time,-day,-week,-month,-or-even-my-friggin'-name kind of way. Because in addition to all this New Mommy stuff, I was still working in the city, recruiting computer programmers and counseling them on hygiene and flatulence. I was so tired, I think I told some guy to stop washing his suits at the office and make sure he farted at least twice a week. Thank God for my boss, Charlie. He let me work from home when I needed to and never said a word when I fell asleep under my desk. Or about the breast pump that had become part of my office décor.

I had long known about the many benefits of breastfeeding: it boosts your child's immune system, strengthens the bond between mother and baby, and the list goes on and on. However, there are also some very definite drawbacks, such as wet spots on your shirt and having to whip a boob out at inopportune moments. I was therefore very much on the fence and leaning toward "thanks, but no thanks." That was until I learned that breastfeeding also helps you lose the baby weight. Decision made. And it was great—until I found myself pumping my breasts on the West Side Highway in rush-hour traffic, praying like hell that a truck didn't pull up next to me. But I figured it was better than walking into a meeting looking like I had sprung a leak.

Joe was exhausted, too. But he had gone through this before with his boys, so I knew he had the stamina and the stomach for it. No matter how busy he was, he'd been there to coach their baseball and football games, and I knew he'd do the same for our kids. And he did from the minute Ariela was born.

No matter what, he still had a sense of humor. Like the night I had a Goldman Sachs dinner at Asia de Cuba, a swanky, Asian-Latino fusion restaurant in Manhattan. It had been a long week and a very long day, and by ten o'clock I was about to pass out in my flan. So when I saw Roy (a guy from Joe's studio whose crazy, blond locks put his Hair to shame) walk past my booth, I thought I was hallucinating.

"Roy?"

The guy stopped and smiled, and I saw it was indeed Roy. WTF? Of course the suits I was with were sitting there with their mouths hanging open. I could just imagine what they were thinking: *I didn't know Dee Snider's making a comeback*, or, *Wow, Lauren really does know all different kinds of people.* Or, most likely, *Can this guy afford to eat here?*

Me and my sisters

Family and friends at the Jersey Shore, Aug 4, 1977. (Clockwise from left: Deena, Claudine, Jeffrey, Lauren, Joey, Suzanne. In the middle: Doug.)

High School Prom

Swimming in the ocean

Jersey Shore night out!

Charlie's Angels

High School Graduation

Me in St. Bart's

Joe at St. Bart's

Joe at the Jersey Shore

Ariela's first and only pony ride in Hilton Head

Danny playing ice hockey in the house

Duchess of York Sarah Ferguson and me

Me and Sir Richard Branson

Me and former
President George
Bush

Me and former President
Bill Clinton

Rocco Dispirito and me with an advance copy of my book.

Backstage at *Lucky Guy!* (Back row) Me, Jenny West, Joe, and Tom Hanks. (Front) Leslie West.

Me with Dr. Oz

Me and Joe in the Cayman Islands

Roy, who saw their expressions, was enjoying every minute of it. Just like Joe's Hair did when they were stopped in the airport. Or on the bullet train. Or on the street while giving a guy a dollar for something to eat.

"Hey, Lauren. Joe and Ariela are in the limo outside. I said I'd come in and look for you."

No sooner were the words out of his mouth than I saw my husband and daughter—who wasn't wearing any shoes or socks—walking toward me. Silly me, I'd thought they were home, asleep. Like I wished I was. Instead it was ten p.m. and I was listening to Joe proudly telling my clients that Ariela had become the first baby to attend an Upper East Side Columbus Club meeting. What he didn't tell them was that he'd refused to hire a babysitter because he was afraid they would steal our daughter. (I liked to remind him that even if they did, they'd return her after a few sleepless nights.)

It turned out all you need to bring an endless business dinner to a close are a shoeless baby and two guys who look like rockers. On the ride home, Ariela was wide awake (and would be for most of the night). I, however, was dead to the world.

# 27

# George, Danny, and My Life as the Nanny

—

After Ariela was born, I wondered whether I'd still be able to go on trips with Joe. I mean, who doesn't know a kid who whines, "Are we there yet?" after five minutes in the car? But as I would soon find out, my daughter was a natural jetsetter; it was everyone else who would have to adjust.

Ariela was only eighteen months old when we took her to Europe for the first time (which meant that between her and the jetlag, we would get even less sleep than usual). Our friends were getting married in Italy and asked us if she could be in the wedding. From the moment we left for the trip, there was no doubt that Ariela was quite comfortable. Particularly with flying, it seemed, because she spent the entire flight to Milan on the pilot's lap, helping him at the controls—as if she needed any confirmation that she already ran the world. Have you ever been annoyed by a crying child on a plane? Well, next time, just be thankful the kid's not in the cockpit.

If you don't believe me, you have clearly never flown Alitalia, an airline so lax they'd let Charles Manson onboard as long as he kissed everyone on both cheeks and gave them a box of cannoli. However, this was before 9/11. I guess as long as she didn't have more than three ounces of baby formula on her, she'd still probably be making friends in the cockpit.

We arrived in Italy safely and, in Ariela's case, refreshed and ready for action. We were staying in Portofino, at the Hotel Splendido. Portofino is one of the most spectacular places I have ever seen, full of lush greenery, views of the sea, and a love of history so deep they haven't even built a new home there since 1935. So it's my guess they didn't appreciate an eighteen-month-old drawing on their walls with a crayon. A reincarnation of Leonardo da Vinci she was not.

I wanted to think my daughter was inspired by all the beauty around her. Joe thought I was nuts and suggested we get her out of the hotel for a while. Finally I agreed, and we put her in the stroller and went for a walk along the cliff, a spectacular stretch overlooking the sea. And, as most cliffs are, really high up. It's not like you can just take an elevator down when you get tired of walking, either—even when your thigh muscles feel like they're going to burst into flames from schlepping a baby and a stroller down three-hundred very steep steps. But that's what we did, and we were so proud of ourselves at the bottom. Until Joe froze mid-smile and pointed behind me. At the friggin' *road* running alongside the stairs.

To me, my daughter's ease with travel was inherited from both of us (in other words, it lent credence to my "genes in a blender" theory). Unfortunately she was also quite happy to carry on my "You Blend" tradition, as well—like in *My Cousin Vinny*, when Marisa Tomei turns to the black-leather-clad Joe Pesci and says, "Yeah, and you blend." The next day, when we were sitting in the Duomo for the wedding mass, I was already trying to recover from my own *faux pas*, also known as forgetting to bring a shawl to wear over your hot Versace dress. The stares I got from the Italian women ranged from curiosity ("Did she grow up under a rock?") to disdain ("Typical American! No respect for tradition!").

While I was attempting to shrug off (no pun intended) my embarrassment, Ariela was looking around the cathedral in awe. And apparently confusing it with the palace in Disney World. It was filled with a perfect, peaceful silence you would expect in a holy place—a place for nothing but the hushed whispers of the devout and the reverent tones of the priest. Or, in this case, a small, high, and surprisingly clear voice that said, "Daddy! Where is Mickey Mouse?" That's the thing about these old cathedrals: everything echoes. The good news was it took the attention off my dress.

After the wedding, we drove back to Milan, where we had booked a suite at the Hotel Principe Di Savoia. Joe had a factory in Milan, and he stayed there whenever he was in town for business. Everyone knew him there, meaning they had accepted him as a law-abiding citizen capable of paying his tab. We were expecting a few days of relaxing by the pool, gazing at the art-covered walls, and (because carbs consumed in Italy don't count) eating huge bowls of pasta. We were *not* expecting the Italian Film Festival or the sea of paparazzi camped out with their cameras, waiting to invade the privacy of the rich and famous. Even Joe and his Hair didn't get much attention that day. He went to check us in while I played with Ariela in the lobby.

I'd been running into celebrities for years, ever since Joe and I had started dating. Some, like Sting, took away my power of speech; others were no big deal. But the one I had wanted to meet the most (aside from Gopher, of course) was George Clooney. And I felt I deserved to; I'd had a crush on him since *The Facts of Life*, for crying out loud! (And if you don't believe he was on *The Facts of Life*, Google it.) Clooney spent a lot of time in Italy, and so did we. Was it too much to ask that we'd run into him? I didn't think so. But years passed, and the closest I had gotten to Clooney was the driver who had claimed to be his BFF so he could squeeze a few extra lire out of me.

I had envisioned many scenarios of how I would meet George Clooney, and all of them involved me looking incredibly stunning, as well as being well-versed in not only his film creds but his social and political activism (he was usually wearing a tux, and the James Bond music was playing in the background). Not one of them included him walking into the Hotel Principe Di Savoia when I was running around after an inexhaustible eighteen-month-old on a quest to find Mickey Mouse. I watched him saunter across the marble-floored lobby, my mouth hanging open. Somehow it didn't matter one bit that he was wearing a gray t-shirt and jeans. It did matter that I was wearing workout pants and an extra large t-shirt of my husband's since my daughter vomited on the car ride over. I'm sure anyone at the hotel would probably have thought I was the nanny.

It's moments like these when you know God indeed has a sense of humor. And He wasn't done laughing at me yet, because a few minutes later, as my husband was showing Ariela off to everyone and his brother, I had a close encounter with another celebrity. Danny DeVito was there, and it was the first time I'd ever looked a man right in the eye (being five-foot-one, this rarely happens to me).

The conversation went something like this:

Me: "I'm from Jersey, too."

Him: "Are you here alone?"

Me: "No, I'm here with my husband and my daughter. See, that's them over there." (Insert wave at Joe so DeVito believes I am indeed attached.)

Me (loudly): "Uh, Joe . . .?"

Later that night we went to the bar for a drink. Joe was dressed like royalty. My husband has many layers; he can go from suspected criminal to international man of business in about two minutes flat. I love this about him. Unless I am underdressed, and we are surrounded by movie stars. George Clooney was there, and Sting. Danny DeVito was also there, smoking a rather large cigar. I looked over at my husband, holding court and having a ball. For once You Blend was actually blending. Me? I tried to join them, but when I tried to drag a chair over, it weighed like three hundred pounds. I would've kept trying, but I was carrying Ariela and it was impossible with only one free hand. That was when I saw Clooney and Sting glance at Ariela, then back at each other as if to say, *What is this kid doing in a bar at ten p.m.? If that was my nanny, she'd be outta here.*

So not only did George Clooney think I was the nanny, but he thought I was a bad nanny. I wanted to say, "The kid doesn't asleep anyway, for crying out loud!" Instead I decided it was time to head up to the room. As I turned to leave, I heard George Clooney say to DeVito, "Hey, Danny, trying to prove something to the women with those big cigars?"

# 28

# Fish out of Water . . . Literally

———

My friend Sharon sent me an email recently in which she referred to me as "PB perfect." By PB she's means Palm Beach. I had to laugh, because this doesn't begin to describe my complicated, sometimes wonderful, but sometimes humiliating history with Palm Beach.

I first went to Palm Beach when I was still working and before I had kids (and graduated from body odor and international visas to dirty diapers and breast pumps). The company held its annual meeting at the Palm Beach Ritz-Carlton—as it turns out, nothing like the one in Manalapan, New Jersey. We always had a few hours off, and some of us would take a taxi into Palm Beach proper. It was only about a thirty-minute drive, but it was a world away. I would sit in the back in utter awe. En route, the taxi driver would give us the lowdown on who lived where. It read like a tour of the Fortune 100: Oprah, Rod Stewart, James Patterson, Susan Lucci, Estee Lauder, Jimmy Buffett.

"And over there you got the owner of Nextel . . ." He'd point out the window, sounding almost as if he knew them. It was just like the guy in Italy. They all had the same spiel. Some sort of International Code of BS, I guess. And it worked on gullible tourists like yours truly and associates. (Later I found out this guy was also totally full of it.)

After the tour, my associates and I would walk along Worth Avenue (which is Palm Beach's answer to Rodeo Drive in Beverly Hills or Fifth Avenue in New York City). Can you say "out of place"? I might as well have had a sign on my head announcing I am from the Jersey shore. Which you might think is weird after all the traveling I had done—flying on the Concorde, staying in five-star resorts across Europe, and hiring oompah bands to play on yachts—but it was true.

Like those cities in Europe, Palm Beach has no shortage of high-end boutiques. When I saw Hermès, I figured I'd get Joe a tie. As soon as I walked into the store, I felt eyes on me: it was the sales associate, who clearly thought I'd be better off at Target or maybe, on a good day, Macy's, which was right over the bridge in West Palm, and who did I think I was, daring to step into Hermès? I felt like Julia Roberts in *Pretty Woman* when she tried to go shopping without Richard Gere. I expected her to come over at any minute and tell me I might as well leave because it was obvious I couldn't afford anything.

My righteous indignation continued until I saw how much the ties were. I actually could have afforded one—several, in fact, if I were willing to decimate my paycheck. But who was I kidding? Joe was more Howard Stern than Hermès, with his jeans, black wife beaters, gold chains, and bracelets (which he'd had specially made and engraved with the name of his band), a baseball hat over his Hair, and high-top sneakers.

But a girl can dream, and in my dream, I, like Julia, would buy the ties from someone else, then return to say to the snotty salesgirl, "You work on commission, right? Big mistake. *Huge.*" I took the thirty-minute taxi ride back empty-handed but with my paycheck intact. Still in complete and utter awe.

Later, we would take some of our favorite family vacations in Palm Beach. And although we were staying at the Four Seasons, we knew it wasn't quite the same as fitting in. On each trip, You Blend and I would go around with our realtor, looking for a vacation home. But they were always in places far south: Highland Beach, Delray, and Gulfstream. These areas are all very nice, but they're nothing like Palm Beach. I still had to stop my mouth from hanging open every time we drove around there.

Something always inevitably happened to let us know we were like fish out of water in perfect Palm Beach. In case we didn't get the subtle hints, sometimes the message was a bit more literal. My stepsons often came along on these trips, and one day Joey and his girlfriend decided to rent a convertible and take a drive up A1A into Palm Beach. It's a stretch of highway that runs along the Atlantic Coast, famous for its beautiful views of the ocean . . . and of the homes of the rich and famous. They drove along slowly, only twenty-five miles an hour, so they could take it all in. Shades on, top down, and music blaring, cruising past Donald Trump's Mar-a-Lago.

Suddenly a humongous fish came from the sky and smashed Joey on the side of the head. It then bounced off him, smacked his girlfriend in the face, and returned for another round. After managing to keep control of the car, which, let's face it, is pretty amazing considering he was just attacked by a flying fish, he pulled over to the side of the road. Some people might think this was a sign from God. But not when you're from Jersey. His first thought was, *Who the fuck just threw a fifteen-pound fish on my head?*

The fish, mind you, was still alive. Joey picked it up, jumped the sea wall, placed it back in the ocean, and then walked back to the car. Which was rented. And now filled with fish scales. The same scales covered Joey and his girlfriend's clothes and faces. They turned around and went back to the hotel. The fish, like the salesgirl in Hermès, seemed to be sending the message that we simply didn't belong in Palm Beach.

# 29

# The Littlest Angel

———

We were at our house down the shore when I found out I was pregnant again. And maybe because we were in the place that had so many child-hood memories for me, my fantasies immediately kicked into overdrive. I had grown up with three sisters, and we'd shared everything (including, unfortunately for me, clothes and other assorted hand-me-downs; I don't think I had my own clothes until I went away to college—maybe). We would have murdered each other over a favorite shirt, the phone, makeup, or a piece of costume jewelry. But we shared a lot of good things, too, like talking about boys or collectively praying that we did not turn into our mother (the verdict is still out on that one), and visiting each other at college. Three of us were even pregnant at the same time!

And this is what I wanted when I had a family: two daughters. They'd get their nails done together, talk on the phone for hours, and be each other's maids of honor. It was everything Joe and I had talked about at the Plaza Athénée on that first trip to Paris. And in keeping with our *tchotchke* tradi-tion, I bought two little angels to give him the news. I had even named this second child: Julia.

Nearly five months in, I was still sick as a dog. Still working. Still exhausted. Still relying on my morning allotment of caffeine to keep me awake (and keep me from barfing) on the train. And very much looking forward to my next visit to the OB/GYN because I was hoping she'd be able to tell me the sex of the baby. Ariela was only ten months old at the time, and as I sat in the waiting room, gently pushing and pulling her stroller, I figured it would be a nice age difference for two sisters. I was still thinking that as I lay down on the table for the ultrasound.

My first clue that something was wrong was the look on the tech's face.

The second was when she said, "Lauren, I am not finding a heartbeat."

There are many ways to tell this part of the story: all of them involving clichés. "State of shock." "Heart-stopping." "Everything went black." "The sky was falling." Take your pick because they're all equally inadequate.

At the time, Joe was in Europe for a trade show and traveling from country to country. When I called, he was on the bullet train with a bunch of colleagues. The connection lasted just long enough for me to sob, "Joe, the baby died," and then the phone dropped out. For the next three hours, he was in a dead zone. No calls in or out.

Still in shock, I scheduled the D&C for the next day and went home. When I got there, my stepson Jeffrey was standing in the driveway as if he'd had some eerie premonition that was now confirmed by the look on my face. I was glad he was there, but all I wanted was to talk to Joe. I must have tried him a million times only to get his voicemail.

But the truly horrible thing, and something that had never occurred to me, was that Joe had thought I was talking about Ariela. I cannot even imagine how he had felt, thinking our daughter was dead and unable to get in touch with me. To this day, I hear from people who were on that train about how he completely and utterly lost it.

That night I sang Ariela her favorite song and rocked her to sleep as I had done so many times before. And I cried for the child I had lost, for the sibling she would never have. I was only grateful she was too young to remember this awful day. Joe called the minute he got phone service, and within hours he was on the Concorde so he'd be home in time for my appointment.

Joe and I consider ourselves pros at dealing with unexpected bumps in the road . . . most of the time. But this was on a completely different level, and we handled it the best we could. I was almost twenty weeks pregnant, and we had ultrasound images. We still have them. We both grieved for the baby that we didn't have, and I treasured the time I had with Ariela all the more. This was the beginning of what I called my "slow down" phase—I stopped trying to do it all. I hired an assistant and cut myself some slack, spending less time in New York so I could focus on what was really important to me: my family. While were still sad about our loss, I was able to cry and move on, and I even admitted that I enjoyed being able to have a glass of wine and travel with just one rambunctious toddler instead of a toddler and an infant.

The doctor couldn't tell me why I had lost the baby beyond "these things happen sometimes." It wasn't until years later, when one of my sisters had a late-term miscarriage, that we found out the real reason: Factor V (pronounced as "five"), a disorder that often causes miscarriages. My sisters and I all have it, which blew our minds considering we'd come from a family of five and already had healthy pregnancies. As awful as it was, it was a relief to find out what the problem was.

The two figurines I gave Joe are at our beach house, and I believe it's no coincidence that I happened to choose angels.

# 30

# Off to Meet the "Wizard"

The next time I thought I was pregnant, I wasn't taking any chances. Call me superstitious, but I went back to the same CVS I had gone to when I was pregnant with Ariela; I peed on the stick in the same bathroom; and I went down the same *tchotchke* aisle and picked out a similar ceramic baby for Joe. I looked for the same cashier, but she wasn't there. Oh well. I had done what I could.

My dreams of having another daughter had even managed to resurrect themselves. Once again, visions of mani-pedis and maids of honor danced through my head. But again it was not to be—this time, thank God, for a completely different reason.

When I found out I was having a boy, I literally burst into tears. Not only because a lifelong dream wouldn't be coming true, but for the simple fact that I had no idea what I would do with a boy. I also felt bad for Ariela; she would never get to share those girly experiences with a sister. I remember asking the nurse to close the door so I could cry. To leave me alone with my misery. She stayed, at least long enough to say, "I understand how you feel. I have a boy."

I joke about it now, but at the time I was scared to death. I'd never had to deal with a crazy boy in my house (my older brother was pretty calm, as well as outnumbered by us girls). But I had certainly heard stories of the kinds of things boys pull. Including my husband's two sons. Like how one of them enjoyed spraying hairspray with one hand and holding a lit cigarette lighter in the other. Until the day he bent over while doing this and burned off both his eyebrows. Or his brother sticking his head between the spokes on the fire escape and getting it stuck there until the police came to cut him loose. One of the boys had even called his teacher a fat ass and Joe had to run to school to smooth things over.

Then there were the stories of *Joe* growing up. How he had gotten a hold of his father's hammer and broken all their neighbors' windows. For fun. Or when, at the age of five, he had rewired the house with live wires. (Can you say evil genius?) My husband actually thought it was normal that he received a gun for his Holy Communion (which, when you think about it, is kinda funny in a Vito Corleone sort of way, but didn't ease my mind in regard to having a son). Later, Joe was on the rifle team at school. But not only was he on the team; he was allowed to bring his own rifle to school with him.

One day at school, Joe and a group of boys measured their penises in the coat room to see whose was the longest, only to get caught by the teacher, who I'm sure wanted to curl up under the nearest coat and die. I also heard about the boys having to walk around with books in front of their crotches after staring at the teacher's boobs.

Joe had two brothers, and one of his favorite pastimes was to stuff one of them into a garbage can, then send him rolling down a hill until the kid threw up. To Joe and his brothers, this was considered *fun*. They were the kind of boys that make me question how the human race has survived so long.

I knew there were the other kinds of boys—ones like my brother and his son. These boys are delights to their parents and teachers. Parent-teacher conferences and report cards are things to look forward to rather than to dread. You can drop these boys off for play dates or birthday parties without worrying that someone will wind up injured, dead, or incarcerated. These boys do not make weapons out of everything and anything, nor do they make scenes at airports, stores, and movie theaters. They also do not end up in the hospital during every vacation. No, these boys like to read books and are able to sit calmly at church. On long car trips, they sit and stare contemplatively out the window. They do not know what the inside of the principal's office looks like, and they talk about their real pets, not the ones they make up for the teacher's benefit.

*Maybe*, I thought, drying my tears after the nurse left the room. Maybe my son would take after my side of the family and be like my brother rather than his father. *Yeah, right.*

Not that I didn't have every reason to hope. My second pregnancy was really easy. He didn't kick much at all. So little in fact that each time I went to the doctor, he'd have to check the ultrasound to make sure the baby was okay. And each time I'd say to myself, "All right, healthy but calm. This seems like a good sign."

*Yeah, right.*

No matter how smoothly a pregnancy is going, there's always stuff you have to contend with. Especially when you're about to give birth, like, any minute. I was due to have the baby on March 24. On March 19, Joe and I had to attend a trade show at the Waldorf Astoria. Trying to make things easier on myself, I made an appointment to get my hair done there rather than running to my usual place. It was the Waldorf, I figured, how bad could it be? Really friggin' bad, apparently. Because I came out of the salon with the worst hair ever. I remember feeling like I had a golden helmet on my head. Cramming a nine-months-pregnant body into a formal gown was fun, too.

So then we were at the event, along with literally a thousand other people. We were squashed in like sardines, and I was the biggest one of all. Just as the speeches began, my son maneuvered himself into a position where he was pressing on my bladder. Very hard. So now I was trying to get through the crowd to get out of the room and to the ladies' lounge. Except no one would move for me. It was like the D train at rush hour.

I was concentrating so hard on holding it in that for a moment I didn't realize the speaker had interrupted his speech and ordered the crowd to move. For me. The pregnant woman with the bad hair. I had thought the worst thing that could happen was I'd pee all over my gown. But that turned out to be the second-worst thing. The worst was having a room of elegantly dressed people part like the Red Sea so I could go to the john. I was so mortified that I didn't return to the event.

I think the Waldorf incident was a sign that I would often be the recipient of unwanted attention in the future (in other words, once my son arrived). The next sign I got (and the one that turned out to be another accurate predictor) was when Danny was born facing backward. A posterior birth, it's called, which is a polite way of saying that during labor you feel the pain in your ass. I tease Danny that he was born a pain in the ass and nothing's changed.

Still, I feel bad about crying when I found out Danny was a boy. Because along with Joe and Ariela, my son is the best thing that's ever happened to me. I am absolutely crazy about him. I will say this, though: he is not your typical kid. In the eleven years since Danny was born, I have spent countless hours trying to figure out just where the hell this one came from. For Danny (who we sometimes call "the wizard,") has become known for doing and saying things I have would never expect from someone so young. Suffice it to say this four-foot-nine child has managed to make an indelible mark not only on me, my husband, and my daughter, but on nearly everyone he meets. I like to think of him as the perfect storm of our gene pool. This revelation came to me in a dream that jolted me awake, and made me jump up straight in bed and say, "Holy shit, this kid is really mine!"

I have friends with perfect, sweet little boys, like my brother and his son. They see Danny, and look at me with pity. I want to say to them, "Pat yourself on the back all you want. It all comes down to genes in a blender."

# 31

# Thank God for Red Wine . . . and Wellbutrin

Having a baby changes you. You have to learn about a whole new world, with its equipment, its customs, and its experts. Then, the second one comes along, and you think, *Oh, I've got this.* I know what I'm doing. It takes maybe a few weeks or maybe a few months before you find out that you have climbed one learning curve, but the new kid puts you at the bottom of a whole new one. Only, in the case of my son, it was more like a learning mountain.

Unlike Ariela, Danny liked to sleep and eat when he was a baby, which at first I thought was a huge plus. It seemed like a relief that he knew what he wanted, that is, until he didn't get what he wanted. Like when we didn't use his preferred brand of nipple for his bottle or if the milk wasn't quite warm enough. Some babies might cry; others, like

Ariela, would refuse to drink it. Not Danny. He found it more efficient to throw the bottle across the room at a speed that would make Andy Pettitte jealous. It was a real pain in the ass to wipe milk off the kitchen wall; on other hand, it was safer than feeding him in the car, where he'd whip it at the driver so hard we'd almost get into an accident. He was like a tiny angry food critic.

While Ariela was a free-spirited artist (because what else could you think about an eighteen-month-old who entertains the pilot on a trip to Milan and redecorates the hotel wall in Portofino?), Danny was more volatile. One day, he refused to take a bath. Like me, my kids have always loved baths; but from that day on, he had a fit every time he heard the tub filling. It kind of reminded me of my old job. Just when I had started to believe my life's purpose was to get unclean males to bathe, I figured it out. We had taken the kids to Universal Studios, and after going on the *Jaws* ride, he thought the shark was going to come up through the drain in the bathtub and get him. I tried telling him that sharks weren't allowed in New Jersey, but he wasn't convinced. And he wasn't taking any chances. Each night he insisted on sleeping with ten stuffed animals around him for added protection. For years, Danny refused to put on a Halloween costume because he was afraid he would turn into the actual character. He'd only wear the yellow raincoat and fireman's hat from DARE. I guess he figured turning into a fireman wasn't as bad as turning into Dumbledore or a Teenage Mutant Ninja Turtle.

All kids have their little quirks, I told myself, but I was totally unprepared for some of his. For one thing, he always looked backward when he ran. This meant the supermarket became a place of horrors, where I was either making sure he didn't lick the handle of the shopping cart if I had him in the cart, or that he wasn't running into food displays or shutting himself in the ice-cream freezer, if I let him loose. He was especially fond of blowing up the fruit bags and popping them. He loved the noise, but what really tickled him was scaring the hell out of everyone in the produce section.

Going out for lunch or dinner was always a treat as well. Usually, after dropping Ariela at dance class, we would go to the local diner. It was tasty, very casual, and—thank God—very loud. We always had the same table, with three chairs and a high chair. The high chair was a climbing structure, and the snaps kept him entertained as he buckled and unbuckled. For Joe and me, it was like a speed-eating contest: a race to eat and get out of there before Danny attracted too much attention. Inevitably, after Danny got bored with the high chair, he would amuse himself by licking either the side of the table or the window if he could get close enough to the glass. After a while, most of the staff knew us (and undoubtedly fought over who had to wait on us), but there was always some well-meaning staff person who thought that maybe the poor little angel was bored. He or she would place a glass filled with crayons on the table. Soon waiters and diners alike would be ducking for cover when he whipped the glass, crayons and all, across the room. What I would do to buy a few minutes of peace amazed me—he once dug tampons out of my purse and played with them as rockets, and I just let it go. When the food arrived (delivered by a now shell-shocked waitress), I'd place Danny on my lap and the pancakes in front of him. He would seem to like them at first but a moment later would turn his nose up in disgust, possibly because he had poured ketchup on them instead of syrup. The grass always looked greener on Joe's lap, but it turned out Danny just wanted to lick each piece of his toast before placing it back in the basket. Then, as if on cue, he'd sneeze on Joe's eggs. Finally, just when I'd be thinking I couldn't take it anymore, Danny would spill water on one of us. Breakfast was officially over. We could never get out of there fast enough, and we always left a really big tip to ease our embarrassment and guilt. A few times I heard a collective sigh of relief as we left and, once, a downright cheer.

Joe and I may have starved to death (or at least been banned from all diners in Jersey) if we hadn't bought each kid a DVD player. After that, we got a precious forty minutes to inhale some food and a glass of red wine, which we needed, because there wasn't one time we left a restaurant that my stomach wasn't in knots.

With two kids now, and Danny such a handful, Joe and I decided I would finally stop working and be with the kids full time. Plus my company had been sold, and the new owners were making me miserable. It seemed the perfect time to leave. But, of course, it wasn't.

Within a few months, Joe's company took a nosedive, complete with factory closings and layoffs. Suddenly, the wonderful Palm Beach vacation home was out of the question—we were lucky we could keep our apartment in Manhattan. Over the next year, Joe would have to let go of nearly half his staff. As bad as the losses and the uncertainty was for us, it was worse for his employees—it was 2001, and people were reeling from the 9/11 attacks and an economic downturn. Things looked pretty dire. It was a tough time, but, as I've said before, we're at our best in tough times.

It took a few years of struggling, but things finally turned around again. Joe's company made a multimillion-dollar deal on a new antidepressant drug, Wellbutrin (or, as we like to call it, "Thank You, Jesus").

# 32

# Paranormal Activity

———

Jerry the Psychic Plumber was right when he said I wouldn't have to worry about money. Just like he was right about everything else. Joe, of course, doesn't want to hear this because, well, let's just say my husband's not a fan of psychics. He thinks they're either spooky or fakes. Then again, there's also the fact that whenever I go to a psychic, it winds up costing him a lot of money. Usually it's thousands of dollars. But there was one time it cost him *millions*.

Which leads me back to Jerry. Because of course it was nice to hear that money wouldn't be an issue. And we were thrilled when the company not only survived, but flourished; it would have been heartbreaking for all Joe's hard work to go down the tubes, and besides, now he got to hire back the people he had laid off, and then some.

But there are other things in life to worry about besides business and money. Like when your very young son returns from a day at summer camp and cannot wait to tell his father that he learned all about sex (including oral and whatnot) from an older kid on the bus. Or when you spend a couple million on a house you don't even like so your kids can be in a great school system, only to find out the place is haunted.

It should have been great. The house had been built in the 1800s and at the time was the largest for sale in Ridgewood, New Jersey. But like I said, I wasn't crazy about it. Not sure why, there was just . . . something. Still, I was determined to make it work. We spent several months (and even more money) renovating the entire place, each and every room. When we were done, it was gorgeous and exactly the way we had wanted it. There was only one problem: I still hated it.

The weird stuff started happening even before we moved in. Every single one of the guys working on the renovations had crazy stories—things moving, noises, that kind of thing. But it was a lot more than that. Whenever I walked into the house, my mood would change drastically. I could be in a perfectly good mood, but as soon as I set a foot inside, I went from wonderful to utterly and irrationally pissed off in the span of about two minutes. This happened *every time.* For a while I thought I was developing late-onset multiple personality disorder. Until I noticed that my son, who was only four years old at the time, seemed to be affected, too. He got cranky and fidgety every time we went there.

On the second night we slept in the house, I felt like someone was watching me. Not just watching, but staring and lurking. Following me wherever I went. (It was kind of like when I was dating Joe, and his Hair was always following us, except his Hair just wanted to hang out, have a few drinks, and pick up a guitar once in a while. Plus it was attached to the most understanding man on earth). I didn't know what this presence wanted, but I didn't think it was anything good.

It just so happened that around that time, my kids' school sponsored a "girls' night out" for the moms. Chitchat, a few hours' break from the kids. I showed up expecting to meet some moms I could hang out with on the playground, the usual stuff. But then I found out that one of the guests was a psychic. *Now we're talking,* I thought. *Right up my alley.*

It wasn't, however, up anyone else's alley. Today, psychics are the "in" thing. They're on TV, helping cops solve crimes and regular people resolve childhood issues. Their books line the shelves of every Barnes & Noble and are just a click away on Amazon. But it wasn't that long ago that if you went to a psychic, people thought you were a step away from *One Flew Over the Cuckoo's Nest.* Luckily for me, I never had a problem with being labeled crazy.

I introduced myself, and the psychic looked at me for a minute or two, then said, "The house you bought is haunted."

And even though I pretty much knew this (and maybe *because* I knew it), I was shocked. But the psychic wasn't done with me yet.

"And your son is afraid to be there."

*Holy crap.*

Soon after that, I visited the neighbor who lived next door and asked if she knew anything about the house's history. It wasn't that I wasn't convinced—more like I needed something concrete to take to Joe. And that was when I really got freaked.

She told me that the original owners had six daughters. None of them got married. Right now you might be thinking, how quaint: the 1800s, the six spinster sisters living together. Sounds very *Little Women*, right? Maybe, except that in this story one of the sisters wasn't so happy about it. She hung herself in the basement, and then decided to stick around to make sure no one else liked living there either. According to my neighbor, no subsequent owners had stayed in the house more than two or three years.

My husband didn't want to hear any of this. And who could blame him? I tried everything to get that ghost to leave, including walking in each room with a lit candle and saying the Our Father. And one night, when I'd really had it, just telling the little bitch to get the hell out, go to the light, do whatever you gotta do, just leave us alone.

She wasn't impressed, and the haunting continued as before. And that was when I turned to my husband and said, "Sorry, hon, but we're outta here."

Some people buy a house and find out there's mold in the basement. I buy a house and find out I have an angry ghost. Ghosts are even harder to get rid of than mold. We put the house on the market and built another one from scratch, where at the least I knew the only nutty history would be ours.

And that's how a fifteen-minute reading ended up costing millions of dollars, and that's also why Joe's not a fan of psychics.

# 33

# Fear of Flying

———

Unlike my family, the Pizzas had accepted Joe's and my relationship from the very beginning; in fact, they welcomed me with open arms. While I was close with both of his parents, his father and I really connected on a spiritual level. Might sound crazy, but that's exactly how it felt. Maybe it was because, like me, Joe Sr. had died and come back—not once but twice. And he got a kick out of talking about it with me.

My father-in-law had two great loves: his family and the smelly cigars he'd smoked for most of his life (and continued to smoke even after he had only one working lung). From the moment I met my in-laws, I could see where Joe got his romantic streak. They had such a beautiful marriage, always holding hands like a couple of kids. They also attended mass together nearly every day and, as regulars, had their own reserved seats in the choicest pew.

Joe Sr. also adored his five children and cried every time he talked about Joe's sister, who had died while just a teenager. She had been given an overdose of morphine in the hospital, and although a nurse had administered the lethal dose, it was actually the fault of the doctor who had prescribed it. (As the story went, the doctor's own son had died in a car accident that week and he was obviously not thinking clearly. He later committed suicide, but whether that was because he was distraught over his son, Joe's sister, or—most likely—both, no one ever knew.)

Ariela was the Pizza's only granddaughter, which of course meant she walked on water. She also bore an uncanny resemblance to Joe's sister's baby pictures and from a young age shared her aunt's artistic flair, which only proved my theory about Ariela's "inspired" artwork on the hotel wall in Italy. The most telling thing was that, by all accounts, Joe's sister had truly been an old soul, like my daughter.

We were in Palm Beach, where we lived each year between December and June, when we got the call that Joe Sr. had been taken to the hospital, and we made immediate arrangements to fly home. This completely freaked me out for two reasons: number one, I was scared to death that Joe's father wouldn't make it (or that he would die before we got there), and number two, because of the dream I'd had the night before.

In the dream we were on a private plane, and something was wrong with it. I don't know what it was exactly, but we were going down. I mean, I could actually feel my stomach dropping. I was praying as hard as I could. *Just stay in the air, just stay in the friggin' air.* Then I woke up sweating like a pig and mentally going through our upcoming trips.

Joe said not to worry about it, it was just a dream, but by then I knew the difference between a regular dream and one of *those* dreams. A prophetic dream. You know, the kind that comes true.

I tried to put it out of my head and had almost succeeded. Until the next night when we were boarding the plane—the *private* plane—to fly back to Jersey. Just like in my dream.

I don't remember exactly when the plane started making an awful noise or began flying like a bird with a broken wing. All I knew was it was even worse than the tin mosquito we had taken to St. Bart's. One look at Joe and I knew he was thinking about my dream. And I wanted to say, "See? I told you so, and would it kill you to just believe in this shit once in a while?" But I was too busy gripping the armrest and praying. Besides, I figured, there would be plenty of time for lectures if and when we landed.

We were somewhere above Virginia when the pilot announced that one of the plane's engines had gone kaput and the other was overheating. We had to land ASAP, much to Danny's disappointment, because he thought this was more fun than the rides at Disney.

Finally we touched down on terra firma, only to wait for another plane. If we hadn't been in a rush to get to Joe's father, we would have rented a car and driven the rest of the way to Jersey. Because, believe me, the last place we wanted to be was in the air. But at least Danny was happy.

When we finally got to the hospital, we found my father-in-law in really bad shape. We spent every minute we could gathered around his bed. A few days later, as we were standing there, he flatlined. Thinking this was the end, I walked over, placed my hands on his head, and started to pray: "Hail Mary, full of grace . . ." Suddenly this bolt of energy went through me. I felt like I was being electrocuted! A second later, the doctors and nurses rushed in, and we had to leave so they could work on him. On my way out of the room, I was tempted to ask them if I could have my own bed—preferably in the psych ward. Instead I called my sister and told her what had happened.

"Josephine, either I just stepped on a live wire or some higher power just went through me." Josephine didn't have any answers, but at least she didn't say I needed to be locked up. Which, in my family, is always a good sign.

My mother-in-law had passed away a few years earlier from a stroke. When she'd died, I'd been there to hold her. I had never done that before, and I'd felt this incredible calmness come over both of us. Looking back, it was the same feeling I'd had that day in the ocean all those years ago. Being there with her made me realize what a blessing it is to be with someone when they take their last breath. Which is why I went to hold my father-in-law's head when he flatlined, only to be zapped by a thousand volts.

I had been honored when Joe and his father had asked me to pick out my mother-in-law's burial clothes and jewelry. I chose the dress she had worn to our wedding, and as I sat in the funeral parlor waiting to give it to the mortician, I stared at the closed door, thinking about my mother-in-law and how much we would all miss her. And I said out loud, "Mom, show me a sign you made it to heaven okay."

Suddenly the door flew open, then slammed shut again. A chill went through me, and I said, "Thank you, Mom. Now let me go get you a shawl."

Feeling better, but still confused as to exactly what had happened with his father, I went to sit with Joe in the waiting room.

We didn't have to wait that long. The doctor came out and, smiling, told Joe that his father was okay. Actually, his exact words were, "Your father's built like a brick shithouse. He's awake and wants to know what we're serving for lunch."

Joe Sr.'s condition continued to improve, and soon he was ready to be released from the hospital. The problem was the doctors didn't think he was well enough to be on his own yet. By then, we had escaped the haunted house and built our own, so we could have him come and stay without being worried that we'd need an exorcist on staff. It was a major event when he moved in, especially since he came with an entourage of ICU nurses and a full-time cook (everything in style; like father, like son).

Ariela and Danny were nine and seven at the time, and they ran over to his "wing" of the house every day to entertain him, which of course he loved. Joe and I went to church with him, or when Joe was traveling, I took him by myself. He stayed with us for a year, and then he went back to his own house, where he lived until he passed away at ninety-one. And it turned out to be a wonderful year, not only for us and Joe Sr., but for my stepson Joe, who married one of the ICU nurses.

# 34

# Palm Beach I: Hair Convention

— ⌢ —

A few years later, we had a house in Palm Beach's Estate Section, which means we were supposed to fit in there now. You can have a house on Mars, but it doesn't mean you're a Martian.

Once we bought our house in Palm Beach, it stopped being a place where I felt like a fish out of water. It was one of *my* places now, and I felt like it became my own personal version of *The Love Boat*. (I like to think of it as an answered prayer or the manifestation of a childhood fantasy.) When I was a kid, the thing I'd loved most about *The Love Boat*, besides Gopher's crisp, white short-shorts, was that all these celebrities were always showing up with broken hearts or some other life issues that could be resolved in sixty minutes. It wasn't that different from Palm Beach. Celebrities are everywhere, although *their* issues are usually resolved by a shot of Botox or a tummy tuck. If I ever saw Vicki standing in front of Neiman's with a handful of leis and the shuffleboard schedule, I'd know I'd died and gone to heaven. For real this time, and on a much bigger boat.

We were going down to Palm Beach to sign papers for the new house and decided to make a vacation out of it. We invited my friend, Sam, to come down for a few days, which I was thrilled about. Sam and I know each other so well that I feel comfortable saying she needs to try a new hair color, and she can list the weird collection of crap I always tote around in my purse, from the half-eaten chocolate chip cookie to the birthday card I never sent to so-and-so to some psychic's business card. But even though she's still one of my closest friends, we don't get to see each other nearly as much as we'd like. We spent most of the time in Palm Beach lying by the pool, drinking, and catching up (or maybe just catching up on our drinking because by that time I had two kids and spent most of my time making sure Ariela ate and Danny didn't light the house on fire).

In any event, combining sun and cocktails can make your mind play tricks on you. I learned that from a life of summers down the shore. So when I first saw the man sitting across the pool from us, I thought I was hallucinating. Because how could my husband be over there when he was just two lounge chairs down from me?

I squinted to get a better look. From a distance the guy could have been Joe. He had on the same black wife beater as Joe, and his Hair was there, too, just hanging out and enjoying the curious stares of bikini-clad passersby with a gorgeous woman sitting next to him. Then "Joe" stood up, and I knew I was going crazy because he was seven feet tall. But the Hair? I had only seen two men with hair like that, my husband and—

That was when Sam said, "Oh, look, it's Beth and Howard!"

As in Beth and Howard *Stern*. Sam wasn't name-dropping. She had grown up with Beth in Pittsburgh and had even dated her brother way back when. She took Joe and me to meet them. After all the years of hearing my husband compared to Howard Stern, it was really weird to see the two of them in the same place. Maybe it was a convention. I expected a bunch of long-haired guys wearing wife beaters and telling dirty jokes to converge on the pool area at any minute.

Howard was friendly but distracted because he was too busy making sure his teenage daughter and her cousin didn't sneak away without telling him. That's the thing about celebrities: underneath the fame, money, and, in this case, flowing black curls, they're dealing with the same annoying shit as everyone else.

# 35

# Palm Beach II: PB Perfect

———

When people heard we'd bought in Palm Beach, they were full of questions, which I guess was their polite way of finding out just how "Palm Beach" we were going to be. They wanted to know whether it was a house or a condo and whether it was in the North End. They replied with a knowing "ohhhhh" when I said, "No, near Worth Ave." Little did they know it was the scene of my Hermès humiliation years earlier.

Suddenly we were living in the Estate Section, an area known for homes that are architectural works of art and a long history of famous residents. My house is down the street from late billionaire John Kluge's estate. Kluge had bought up much of the surrounding property for his compound, so today it's a quiet cul de sac (or is when my son's not around). At the end of the street are two driveways (also courtesy of Kluge) blocked by large, wooden doors that open for residents and their guests. Security cameras are posted outside, and my son and his friend enjoy jumping up and down in front of them while brandishing swords, rifles, and evil grins. I like to say that Danny is mocking all the pomp and circumstance of a privileged world, that he's a man of the people. What I'm thinking is, *Thank God his weapons (unlike my husband's childhood arsenal) are fake*. Except for the evil grin; that's the genuine article.

Jimmy Buffett (or "Fluffett," as my son likes to call him) lives across the street (contrary to what that cab driver had told me years earlier; like Clooney's friend in Italy, he was completely full of it), and James Patterson lives a few blocks away in John Lennon's old house. It was nothing to see Susan Lucci and her mother shopping on Worth Street or a pre-scandal Tiger Woods partying at Catch, a local nightclub. And when we went to the Breakers, which was pretty often, we'd see Matt Lauer in his swimsuit chasing his kids around or Jerry Seinfeld with his family at an Italian restaurant that serves as Palm Beach's version of Chuck E. Cheese.

My young son was doing his best to live up the celebrity hype around him and was starting to make a name for himself. Of course, it was for things like trying to stow away on someone's golf cart, the *someone* being the oldest son of the Breakers' president, or for getting the glue from a light stick in his eye during Thanksgiving dinner. He'd gone to the bathroom only to return in the company of three security guards. No pumpkin pie for us; we spent the remainder of the holiday in the emergency room, giving thanks that the little genius wasn't going to be blind.

Raising a child in Palm Beach is a little different from raising a child in Jersey. And compared to the way I grew up, it might as well have been another universe. When I was a kid, I made fifty cents a day picking up used condoms on the beach. By the age of ten, I'd handled more DNA than *CSI* New York, Miami, and Vegas put together.

In Palm Beach kids have jobs, too. My little entrepreneurs, for example, owned and operated a lemonade stand. Cute, right? Except they were charging $200 a glass. Not that they always got quite that much, because even though people in Palm Beach think nothing of paying a few thousand for a pair of shoes, they do recognize highway robbery when they see it. Still, Fluffett pulled up in his forest-green Bentley and gave Danny a twenty dollar bill (which thrilled my kids to no end), while the owner of the Tampa Bay Buccaneers paid fifty dollars for a glass. After a few hours, during which they had collected actual two-dollar bills from my neighbor and God knows how much else from other local kind-hearted souls, the lemonade was watered down and warm. The little shysters didn't care, though; they would have kept right on selling it if I hadn't shut the whole thing down.

Birthday parties were another shock to my system. When I was a kid, birthday parties were in the house or the backyard. We opened presents, ate cake, and played pin the tail on the donkey. Within a couple of hours everyone had gone home, leaving the birthday kid to help her mother pick up the wrapping paper and clean soda stains off the carpet.

In Palm Beach, kids' parties are worthy of royalty. For one, they're held in a hall (as in a wedding hall) or a country club; some kids take private jets to Disney. (It's moments like these when I think about my great-grandmother coming to America for a better life, which meant living in someone's basement, and say, "WTF?") These events are catered, with waiters and waitresses serving the food. And they usually last at least four or five hours so the guests can saunter in whenever the mood strikes them. Oh, and did I mention that most of the parents attend as well? But no pressure.

Of course if you've been PB Perfect your whole life, these soirées are no big deal. If, however, you're a recovering fish out of water, let me tell you they are a big friggin' deal. The first party I threw down there was for Danny's seventh birthday. We invited the whole family and rented out an entire recreation center. No pin the tail on the donkey for *these* kids; we hired Palm Beach's best balloon artist and magician for their entertainment. Everything was going according to plan until an hour before the party, when I received a call that Palm Beach's best balloon artist had been rushed to the hospital for emergency gall bladder surgery. I was thrown into a complete panic. What the hell was I going to do with a bunch of third graders? If this had happened to my mother, she would have pushed all the kids out of the house (probably in a blizzard, since my birthday is in December) and told us to go play. This is completely acceptable in Jersey. In Palm Beach you have your friend call her friend (who happens to be the daughter of fashion designer Lily Pulitzer), and an hour and a half and an extra $600 later you have Gary the Magician at your doorstep. And since you've said the magic number, namely zip code 33480, Gary *happens* to know another *artiste* who, for an additional $700 dollars, will blow up balloons. I knew it was a rip-off but figured it was money well spent if it ended my panic attack.

That panic reprieve lasted about five hours. The longest party in history was finally drawing to a close, and I was more than ready to give everyone a goody bag and a kiss-kiss on each cheek and send them on their way. That was when I found out that Joe's business partner had brought a goody of his own—an IV bag from a bulk pharmacy filled with a mysterious liquid that he wanted to show Joe. Not wanting to hold it out in the open, he had shoved it in one of the little bags. Didn't know which one, of course, so now, completely freaking out, I was trying as subtly as possible to go through all the bags and find it before one of the guests left with it. I didn't know what would have been worse, a parent finding it or a kid, but I could just hear the conversation:

"Did you hear about the drug dealers who moved down the street from the Kluge estate?" someone would whisper over sushi at Echo or drinks at Taboo. "*Italians* from *New Jersey*."

"Yes, dear, aren't they the ones who put something in little Johnny's goody bag at their son's party? Pharmaceutical business *indeed*."

Thankfully we found the right bag in time. Disaster averted. But, needless to say, for the next party we used clear bags and told Joe's partner to leave any extra bags he had at home.

And in case you're thinking I'm exaggerating about the Italian thing, I'm not. My husband likes to wash his own cars, which is pretty normal when you live in the Tri-State Area, but in Palm Beach not so much. So, one bright, sunny day, he was outside washing his Porsche and decided to play some music while he worked. Actually, *blast* is more like it. And since it happened to be a song he had composed, he was like a pig in shit.

Until he felt a bony finger tapping him on the shoulder. He turned around to find one of our neighbors, a woman in her seventies, glaring up at him. In New Jersey she would have been pissed. In Palm Beach, she was *put out*.

"You know, sir," she said in her best you-don't-belong-here voice, "I must ask you to turn that down. This is a very quiet street, and the owner of this house would not be pleased one bit with you blasting your music."

Joe realized she thought he and his Hair had been hired to wash the car. Luckily, after years of being stopped at airports and treated like a bum in flea markets, my husband had cultivated a certain air of amused calm.

"Well, actually," he explained with a smile, "I *am* the owner, and I wrote this song. It was just nominated for a Grammy, and I'm just really excited. Sorry."

Her demeanor completely changed. In two seconds flat, my husband went from persona non grata to musical genius. The news travelled fast. That night we were invited to a gathering at the lady's house, where we were fawned over by every older couple in the neighborhood. By the time we left, they wanted to sponsor us at the very exclusive Everglades Club on Worth Avenue, which, they were very excited to tell us, had recently started accepting Italians!

Even though we were now homeowners in Palm Beach, we were still fish out of water.

# 36

# Jerks in Caicos

———

Vacationing is something we love to do. There are so many wonderful places in the world to explore, so many amazing sights to see, so many beautiful hotels and houses and to stay in—but for some reason, we can never find them. Joe and I took the kids to Sardinia. It was late summer—the height of the season—and it can get pretty crowded, which is why we were so grateful when our friends generously offered us the use of their place. We could take in all the sights and pig out on rock lobster and pastries without staying in a crowded hotel. Perfect!

From the minute we booked the trip, all I heard from my husband was how unbelievable-looking the Sardinian women are. So exotic, stunning, blah, blah, blah. I mean, really, Joe? It wasn't that I was jealous; I just thought he was exaggerating. How could one place have so many gorgeous women?

When we got there I saw how wrong he was. Because the women were nothing. It was the *men* who were unbelievable. Every single one of them, from the taxi driver to the waiter, looked like he had been dipped in bronze. I twisted my head so much it's a wonder I didn't end up with a serious case of whiplash.

I forced myself to stop gawking and concentrate on Sardinia itself. Next to Sicily, it's the largest island in the Mediterranean, and it's breathtaking. And again I thought, *This is going to be perfect.*

I held that thought until we got to the "villa." I don't know what hit me first, the dungeon-like lighting or the oppressive heat. It was late summer, and no air conditioning. But a thousand times worse than that was the bodies of fat roaches that littered the floor. They were on their backs, feet in the air. You know a place is bad when roaches can't survive. I sat down on the bed only to have my ass hit the ground because the mattress was old as dirt and just as filthy. Joe and I looked at each other like, *Are you kidding me?* It was like a horror movie where the unsuspecting couple goes on a luxury vacation only to find themselves incarcerated in some tropical shithole . . . inhabited by zombies.

If Joe and I were alone, we might have sucked it up, worn flip-flops in the shower, and had a laugh. But I'd be damned if I was going to let my kids be carried off by a brigade of Sardinian insects on a hunting and gathering mission. We were outta there. Easier said than done, since it was high season and all. Joe had to bribe a concierge to get us into a "booked" hotel, but it was gorgeous, overlooking the sea, and free of bugs. That pretty much put an end to staying in people's houses, unless they live there full time.

The vacation that really takes the cake, though, was our trip to Turks and Caicos. December 26, 2009. An 8:00 a.m. flight out of JFK. Which we would have been on time for except for some jackass who had strapped a bomb to his body the day before, because what would the holiday season be these days without a threat of being blown to bits?

So it was after seven, and we were still standing in the check-in line along with a bunch of other pissed-off people, collectively huffing and shifting our weight from one foot to another like that would speed things up. (Because in other places, people would be sighing with relief that the terrorist had been caught. Hugging each other and smiling with gratitude that they would not die in a fiery explosion. In New York, it's like, okay, show's over; now get me on the friggin' plane.)

Finally I ran to the front of the security line and asked if we could go ahead since our plane was about to leave. Joe and the kids—eight and six years old at this time—were among the huffers and puffers, and I didn't want to deal with them if we missed the only flight out that day. The woman I asked must have had a husband and kids too, because she shot me a sympathetic look and said, "No problem, honey."

So we ran like animals through a terminal packed with holiday travelers, with all our bags because it was too late to check them. This really sucked for Joe because, as usual, he had packed half his closet. I would have said "I told you so," but I'd hit a pretty good stride by then and I didn't want to blow it by talking.

Somehow we still found time to get snubbed by Buddy the Cake Boss, who was on the same flight. He didn't remember meeting me at the W Hotel a few weeks earlier (which was fine), but he also wasn't friendly to my kids, who love his show (which wasn't fine). I wanted to tell him he was a jerk; then I remembered that he, too, had gotten up at 4:00 a.m. to schlep his family on a "vacation" only to be nearly blown up and have to run an obstacle course to the gate.

My heart was still pounding when we finally took our seats. And that's why I never book an early morning flight.

But that was just the beginning.

If you Google the resort we had booked, you see phrases like "spectacular luxury" and "dream vacation." American Express gave it one of the highest recommendations, which convinced me I should book it despite the inflated holiday price of $2,500 a night plus tax.

We had all decided to shake off the crappy morning, and by the time we landed in Turks and Caicos we were already laughing about the mad dash through the airport. We held those happy thoughts until we got to the hotel.

It began when we went to check in and the person behind the counter was nasty. In fact, the whole staff was nasty. Then, after waiting around in the lobby (because the words "early check-in" meant nothing here, apparently), we finally climbed the two flights to our suite. Yes, folks, a walk-up. I could have gone on vacation in Brooklyn and I only would have had to get on a train.

The suite itself was okay but not "spectacular" (and certainly not $2,500 worth of spectacular). But who cared? We were on a beautiful island, and we were going to enjoy it despite a nasty staff and so-so suite. And we did. We frolicked on the beach until late afternoon, then we went back to the hotel to get ready for dinner. I couldn't wait to take a nice, long shower and wash off the grime (and the aggravation) of the day. My first reaction when I turned the faucet was to laugh. Not a ha-ha laugh but an I-can't-believe-this-shit laugh. Because there was no friggin' water! I took a deep breath and picked up the phone to call the front desk, but it was busy.

I decided to go down and complain, and I had two flights of stairs to compose myself so I wouldn't yell at the person. Too late for that because there was already a bunch of other people at the desk, yelling that they hadn't had water in days. In that moment, I figured out why the staff was nasty when we checked in. They saw us as people who would no doubt be pains in their asses in the very near future.

I heard the person behind the desk saying it was a problem on the *entire* island. I didn't know if that was true, but it didn't matter anyway because due to the holiday, there were no other hotel rooms available. We went to dinner that night slick with suntan lotion and smelling like seaweed.

By the next morning, everything was as it should have been and water flowed from the pipes. We were so excited to be able to shower and just feel *clean*. Problem solved, or so we thought—until we returned from the beach. Apparently there is no water on Turks and Caicos between the hours of 4:00 and 6:00 p.m. A two-floor walk-up and intermittent water pressure. Like I said, we could have gone to Brooklyn.

We spent the rest of the vacation at the mercy of crappy pipes, racing back from the beach by 2:00 p.m. so we could go out to a restaurant without offending the maître d. Then came the day when we learned the truth. We decided to rent a boat for the day, pipes be damned. When I asked the captain if he had a shower onboard, he looked at me like I was out of my mind. What, didn't he know about the water pressure problem gripping the island?

"Who told you that, the concierge? Everyone knows that resort is one of the crappiest on the island."

I was thinking, *Yeah, thanks, mister. Too bad you don't work for American Express.* But since I wasn't about to piss off a guy with a working shower, I limited my response to a thank-you. The shower was pure heaven.

Other hotels did open up after New Year's Day. There were rooms available for a cool $5,000 a night (because that's apparently what you have to pay to get running water on Turks and Caicos; *my bad*). However, by then we couldn't move because my son and I were in the grips of salmonella from some lobster we'd eaten. We spent the rest of the trip vomiting, shivering in front of the TV, and showering whenever we had water.

The good news was I didn't have to worry about that post-holiday diet. Any weight I had gained—and then some—was effortlessly lost over the next *six* weeks.

# 37

# The Princess and the Pretender

———

Like I said before, my children couldn't be more different from one another. Probably because Ariela is the ultimate girly-girl: she's reserved and private and has been getting facials since she was in diapers. And Danny is the ultimate boy's boy: a cross between Don Juan and Dennis the Menace, with a dash of Andrew Dice Clay thrown in. Yet both kids inherited traits from me, my husband, and scads of wacky relatives on both sides of the family.

Ariela has every bit the fantasy life I did as a kid. But whereas my fantasies stayed safely in my head, in part because I didn't want my family to think I was any crazier than they already did, my daughter acts hers out. As a child, I kissed the TV screen and dreamed of running away with Gopher; Ariela spoke openly with imaginary friends. I saw myself as the heroine in a romance novel; my daughter performs in school plays. To me, the world was a place to escape into myself; to Ariela, the world is a stage, and it makes the most sense when she's in the lead. She sings, too, but that she most certainly got from Joe.

When I was a kid, I would have killed to walk into a store and buy new clothes of my own rather than wearing my sisters' castaways. Ariela, despite being able to have whatever she wants or maybe even because of that, loves to design her own clothes. This talent was passed down from Joe's mother, who once made her living designing wedding gowns. So while my daughter is very grounded and sensible, she also seizes every opportunity to create things according to her vision—such as the time Joe came home without his Hair.

He'd been on the verge of cutting it anyway, but the catalyst was a particularly snooty Upper East Side co-op board whose approval we needed to buy our apartment. And just like that, his Hair—the source of so many airport stop-and-frisks and flea-market bargains—was sentenced to the barber shop floor. Seven-year-old Ariela stared at him for a moment, then demanded he glue it back on. To her, his Hair was simply a theatrical prop Joe used to play his part in the world.

Five-year-old Danny, on the other hand, simply refused to go to him. He wasn't going to be fooled by this short-haired guy who *sorta* resembled his father. Because, unlike his sister, Danny's always taken things quite literally. When I wanted to fix Sam up on a blind date, he asked why I would set such a beautiful girl up with a guy who couldn't even see her. Things like that.

And then there was the time I told him the story of how I'd drowned when I was thirteen. My intention was to teach him that heaven is real and that I was grateful for the experience. My mother had discouraged such talk, but I was determined to do things differently. I wanted my kids to embrace their spirituality. Was that too much to ask? Apparently so, because the next day I went to pick Danny up from school only to find my car surrounded by a bunch of screaming boys. They wanted to know if I was really a zombie back from the dead.

When I had some basal cells removed from my face (effectively ending my Restalyne plans), he told everyone at school I was a cancer survivor and even asked them to wear pink for me. I got so many phone calls that night you'd have thought I had stage four breast cancer, God forbid. For the first five phone calls, I laughed as I explained the truth; by the tenth call, I was answering with, "I have three small stitches and a Band-Aid on my face, okay?"

Danny also has a theatrical side, and his preferred method of acting is whatever will drive everyone absolutely bat shit. At the country club, he ordered six Shirley Temples at once, then staggered around the place, telling his friends—and their parents—that he was wasted. He is constantly faking injuries at school so he can go to the nurse (who has sons of her own and, therefore, a fairly decent BS meter; however, since my son is in her office three or four times a week, she clearly has never dealt with this caliber of BS before). My son has quite an acting career going, and he's continually looking to up his game. What else am I supposed to think when we're in the drug store and he rattles off a laundry list of items he wants, including crutches, a wheelchair, leg braces, medical tape, and finger splints? I pictured him taping up his fingers just so, then flipping the bird to students and teachers alike. And telling them it was a field hockey injury.

My son also has no filter; he says whatever's on his mind. He asked our nanny, who is from Barbados, if she was black because she ate too much chocolate. He insisted on telling me that although his name was on the card, he had *not* been the one to send me the Mother's Day flowers. At a Disney dinner, he threatened to send Pluto to the moon. Joe was away at a tradeshow and I had taken the kids to Disney. Pluto came over and asked if he could take pictures with us. Danny looked up at him and said, "Don't get too close to my mother. She's married, ya know." Pluto shrugged and moved over a little, but my son continued to give the big, yellow dog dirty looks until he left. He also gave the evil eye to the guy who, after doing my nails, made the mistake of giving me a complimentary neck rub while I had my hands under the dryer. I have to admit, I was flattered that Danny looked up from his Game Boy, because nothing makes him do that. At dinner, he told Joe that the man at the nail salon was flirting with me, to which Joe raised an eyebrow, but he knows me . . . and our son.

My personal favorites, though, have taken place at the airport. Once, Danny saw a man with a turban and a long beard and said, "Hey, Dad, it's bin Laden! You gotta call the cops!" Another time, when we were going through airport security, the police asked Danny to fork over the wine opener/pocket knife he was carrying (unbeknownst to us). My son proceeded to raise holy hell, screaming, "It's all the Arabs' fault!"—so loud Ahmadinejad probably heard it in Tehran. And I thought traveling with the Hair had been bad.

Danny also loves animals. He tried to order a horse on the Internet (and pulled out clumps of grass that he stored in the garage so his new pet would have something to eat). At a restaurant in Milan, he fed the pigeons crumbs from the bread basket. After getting yelled at by the owner, he placed the basket down, folded his hands in his lap, and waited patiently. Just long enough for us to forget about it. Then, quick as lightning, he grabbed the basket and flung the remaining crumbs in the direction of the hungry birds. The result was worthy of Hitchcock: pigeons descending upon us (and the other horrified diners) in a frenzy of beaks, wings, and feet. We didn't know whether they were in search of breadcrumbs or human flesh, and we didn't care. We ran like hell and, needless to say, didn't bother returning to that little trattoria.

And, Danny is committed to philanthropy, or at least he pretends to be. He and a friend went around our neighborhood selling cookies to raise money for their baseball team. Except the baseball team didn't need any money, and they had stolen the cookies from my pantry. I had no idea what they were doing and wouldn't have found out if my neighbor hadn't called, asking if she could write me a check for three dollars. When she told me what it was for, my first thought was, *A check for three dollars? What, does she need proof for a tax write-off?* My second thought was that while Danny had inherited his business skills from Joe and me, he'd clearly gotten his business *ethics* from Bernie Madoff.

My son has the makings of either an outspoken political activist or the architect of a Ponzi scheme. Whichever the case, I'll be sure to have the bail money ready.

# 38

# Fifty Shades of Fear

———

I have to admit, I don't have many fears. I guess that's what dying at thirteen does to a person. Committing social faux pas across Europe (and several in Palm Beach) didn't hurt either. But I am petrified that something will happen to my children—my son in particular.

I know you're thinking, *What parent doesn't worry about their kids?* Still, my anxiety goes through the roof if one of them goes out without a cell phone. Why? I could give you some psychobabble about having baggage from my own childhood, and maybe that's true. I think it's more likely that I am anxious because they've given me reasons to be. Ariela once took Tylenol Cold and had seizures, and Danny nearly had his toes torn off because he decided to ride an escalator in the wrong direction at Newark Airport. Once you've watched a security guard wipe down your kid's bloody feet, and searched the airport for shoes to replace the flip flops that had gotten caught in the steel and shredded, you start to look at most everyday things as potentials for disaster.

But like so many other terrifying/humiliating/generally unnerving experiences in my life, most of these scares took place while we were traveling. Before going on vacation, most people like to do a little research on the place, especially if they've never been there before. You know, what there is to do, the names of the best restaurants, and the local flora and fauna—whatever. Me? I ask which hospital is closest to the hotel. Because we will inevitably have a reason to go there. Every time.

Not surprisingly, most of these incidents involve my son. He had a staph infection at Hilton Head and gastroenteritis in Florida. He threw up on the steps of the Duomo in Italy. He threw up every time our plane landed, but that might have been because he'd spent the entire flight booking up and down the aisle like a quarterback headed for the goal line. He almost got blown away in Switzerland, because that's what happens if you run down the halls of La Réserve waving a toy gun when the Saudi prince is staying there. And, just so you know, His Highness's security doesn't care if the "assassin" is only four feet tall and wearing footy pajamas, especially if he's yelling, "I want to meet the real prince!" at the time.

But without a doubt, Danny's had the worst luck at Disney. Basically, if my son is Superman, Disney is a city full of kryptonite. It doesn't matter whether we're talking about Disney World in Florida or Euro Disney in France; he's gotten violently ill in both places. Because while Superman avoids kryptonite at all costs, Danny devours it. The kid had to lick everything. If he wasn't licking a pole on the monorail, he was sucking on a joystick in the game room. *I* nearly barfed just thinking about how many hands touched these things every day. He might as well have been licking the toilet seat of a Port-o-Potty (and would have, if given the chance).

If a stomach virus in Florida wasn't bad enough, the one at Euro Disney landed him in the hospital, which I had already researched and called, introducing myself to the admissions staff and explaining that we'd be coming in at some point over the next week, ETA to be determined by fate and whatever disgusting thing my son chose to lick that day. Before going to the hospital, my son managed to vomit all over the monorail as well as several little girls who had just come from Disney Castle. They were wearing their perfect princess dresses and had just had their hair done (at seventy-five dollars a pop) at the Princess Salon. They were living the fairy tale. Or at least they were until my son threw up on them. Welcome to reality, ladies.

To make matters worse, he also used to bite his nails, probably because he was stressed out about what crappy thing would happen to him next. After warning him a thousand times about germs on his hands and everything else he put in his mouth, I decided that I wouldn't say anything. *Lick the rides*, I'd think. *Make out with the monorail. Just bring on the stomach virus because it's gonna happen anyway.*

The vacation that gave us the biggest scare began without a hitch. No one was stopped by airport security, the plane had two working engines, and the hotel was beautiful and had plenty of water pressure. Danny didn't throw up when we landed, and he'd even resisted the temptation to lick the window of the taxi. Still, I was waiting for the other shoe to drop because it always does.

I don't know how my son got the scrape on his arm; it was less than a centimeter long, so it couldn't have been too dramatic an event. Yet somehow, two days later, Danny had a full-blown case of MRSA (Methicillin-resistant *Staphylococcus aureus*). We spent the next five days in the hospital, praying that the heavy-duty antibiotics worked before the bacteria could eat away at his bone. For my son, though, it was business as usual. Licking everything he could reach from his hospital bed—the TV remote, the bed rails—and torturing everyone around him.

So it's no wonder that I worry. Some of my worries have nothing to do with Ariela and Danny, but rather with the world today. I mean, it doesn't take a rocket scientist to see that things are completely different from when I grew up. And that's true whether you live in South Jersey or the south of France.

When I was a kid, Atari was considered high tech, and if boys wanted to see a naked woman, they had to break into their fathers' secret stashes of *Playboy*s. Today, kids video chat with their friends (and God knows who else) long after their parents are asleep, and my son and his friends were Googling "girls' boobs" before the age of ten.

There's just no way to stay on top of everything. Everyone's business is exposed for all the world to see. Like our friends who were—for lack of a better word—sexting each other. They're a married couple, so what's the big deal? Well, the big deal was that their three daughters got to the phone before their mother. And read their father's text—"Honey, I am so horny 4 U"—out loud.

You can just imagine the conversation after that ("Mommy, what does *horny* mean?" "It's a bad word, honey." "But then why is Daddy texting that to you?" and so on). But because I wanted to make my friend feel better (and remind her that, as the mother of three girls, she still had it easier than I did), I said, "That's nothing. Try going into your kid's iPhone and seeing a collection of nudes. And I'm not talking about Henri Matisse or Paul Cézanne. These pics were downloaded from a website that makes Girls Gone Wild look like Girls Gone to Church."

We've all heard the saying "you can learn something from everyone." Well, after looking at this site, I can say without a doubt that it's the truth. It provided me with quite an education (lesson one being don't let your kid have Internet access). Oh, and PS for all you unsuspecting and technologically dysfunctional parents out there: you cannot just delete these sites from the phone. To get rid of them, you have to take it to the Apple store and have their people remove it and put on the parental controls.

Joe and I had another techy near miss, this one with the family iPad. The kids are supposed to read thirty minutes each night; we actually have to write it down in a log and give it to the teacher. Joe and I had downloaded a ton of books on the iPad, so we figured it was a great way to get them to read without hearing excuses about losing the book, leaving it at school, whatever. So we put some of their books on our iPad and it worked really well until the night Joe asked Danny what he was reading.

"*Fifty Shades of Black*," he answered innocently.

I thought Joe was going to have a stroke. We found out, thank God, that he was lying. Besides getting the title wrong, he told his father it was a book about kids who lived in a swamp. Total bullshit but still too close for comfort. And that was when both kids got Kindles of their own, complete with parental controls.

Xbox Live seemed like a great invention, too, especially when I found out my son had made a new friend. *How cute*, I thought. Then he told me the friend was a thirty-year-old man from DC who referred to himself as the N-word. Yes, of all the names in the world, he chose that as his handle. And my son thought this guy was so great that I might actually want to talk to him—an offer I politely declined.

I could be stressed out about this stuff twenty-four/seven. But inevitably someone comes along who has it even worse, as another friend recently reminded me. She was at Disney with her three children and her parents. Sounds lovely, right? Yeah, until she walked into the room to find her kids watching porn just a few feet from the couch where her mother lay sleeping in blissful ignorance. Once again Disney had proven itself to be a vortex of evil. If I had my way, they'd burn some sage to cleanse the place, or at least have a parent support group. Then again, it would probably be run by Mickey Mouse.

# 39

# The C-Word

When I found out my mom had breast cancer, my first reaction was blind panic. My second was to say, "Dammit, Mom, if you ever went to the friggin' doctor you would have caught this earlier." And my third thought was that "they"—the spirits that have always guided me—were conspicuously absent. I'd dreamt of September 11; I saw the seas rising up and colliding before Hurricane Sandy. But with my own mother's health, nothing. But I didn't dwell on it because I was too busy praying.

After the first saw-happy surgeon recommended a mastectomy, we made an appointment at Sloan-Kettering. I knew my mom was scared (meaning she got choked up for about a second), but she was holding it together (meaning she insisted on staying in my apartment in the city the night before so we could beat the morning rush from Jersey).

The night before her surgery, I took her to a French restaurant for dinner, partially because I wanted to cheer her up, but also because it's mentioned in *Happy Birthday*, the new Danielle Steel novel I'm reading. (If you've read one Danielle Steel book, you've read them all, but I couldn't resist, especially since it's about a talk-show host who goes to a palm reader.)

We were both scared out of our minds, but determined not to let it show—we were in for a battle and were going with full armor. We lost my grandfather to cancer, so we didn't have any illusions that this would be easy. Running through my mind were medicines . . . side effects . . . baldness . . . cure . . . and I know she was thinking all of this, too.

Bright and early the next morning, my sisters were at my door to take us to the hospital. One of the first things the doctor asked us was if we had any cancer in the family. When I told him about the basal cell I'd had removed from my face, I caught my mother and sisters rolling their eyes at each other. Then my sister Josephine pulled out her phone and began typing something. I didn't give it too much thought because, thank God, the doctor was telling us that although Mom had a rare and aggressive form of cancer, she could get away with a lumpectomy.

He wanted to run more tests, so they sent us back to the waiting room. The first thing my mother did was call my father to give him the good news. This was the man who had dropped her off at the curb for each baby because he didn't have the stomach for any medical stuff. When he asked my nana to take her—probably because he didn't want to hear Mom panting the whole way—she got pissed and just drove herself. She was talking too loudly, and I was thinking, *Why don't you just open the window and yell toward New Jersey?*

Josephine was once again typing frantically. I was only half serious when I asked, "Are you writing another screenplay?"

She leaned over and handed me the phone so I could see that yes, she was in fact making notes for a new script. It had just about everything we'd said and done all day: how despite the situation my mother still thought to pack a red outfit for Valentine's Day and how I kept complaining about my left boob (I had a sympathy pain, for crying out loud!) and told Mom not to worry about losing her hair because I'd get her extensions.

I was a little annoyed at my sister, but it could have been worse. The last time Josephine wrote me into one of her movies, I had an STD from a cheating ex. I spent the entire film festival explaining to everyone and his brother that it was most definitely fiction.

Mom made it through the surgery and is now cancer-free, but I never heard what happened with Josephine's screenplay. . . . I hope Reese Witherspoon plays me!

# 40

# "How Things Are Done"

My longtime friends—those who knew me when I wore my hair like Melanie Griffith in *Working Girl* and thought Asti Spumante was the height of sophistication—are always amazed by my ability to embrace new people and situations with a sense of calm (and a handful of Xanax). Let's face it: I went from a working-class environment where you've "arrived" if you can take your kids on one vacation a year to socializing with the fabulously wealthy and outwardly perfect.

When I started dating Joe, I wasn't just introduced to luxury; I was introduced to a lifestyle. And with this lifestyle came a list of rules—how things are done. And if you don't do things how things are done, you face consequences that range from being a cocktail-party joke to being an outright social pariah.

This pressure to look, act, and speak a certain way can be a bit overwhelming, particularly if you grew up on a steady diet of guidos, cheesy novels, and even cheesier TV. But for some reason (I'm not sure, but I think it was the drowning incident—I guess that's what dying does to a person), I am blessed with the ability to shake it off and move on, usually to the next humiliation or—if I'm on vacation—the next hospital trip with Danny.

"How things are done" includes what to say, what not to say, and when to keep your mouth shut altogether, which, given the fact I grew up in New Jersey, is a completely foreign concept to me. I have an impressive ability to stick my foot in my mouth . . . and down my throat. Once, when we were talking to some good friends, I mentioned how we had been at a luncheon with Robert De Niro. I went on and on about how we had actually spoken to him and how it's hard to reconcile that this guy played both the tattooed psycho rapist in *Cape Fear* and the weepy don in *Analyze This*.

They listened to my story, politely nodding and even adding "ooh"s and "ahh"s in all the appropriate places. I later found out they were De Niro's partners in one of his restaurants, Tribeca Grill. After I heard this, and confirmed it with a Google search, I replayed the conversation in my head. I remembered the polite nods and "ooh"s and "ahh"s. My friends from Jersey would have cut me off at the knees, both to put me in my place and to help me save face. So why had they let me go on like a schmuck? Simple: because they are kind, gracious people and consider it rude to interrupt a friend. It is not "how things are done."

This may come as a shock (insert sarcastic smirk here), but I believe that sometimes it's just better to let it out. When my friend showed up on my doorstep wearing the ugliest shoes I had ever seen, I let her know. They were big, clunky things with rubber soles and a mess of ribbons and clips securing her feet in place. She saw my glance, as well as my shudder, and explained, "I know they're ugly, but they're the latest rage—and so comfortable." And I thought about how it is done and though, *Screw that*.

"They are hideous!" I burst out. "Just hideous!"

I've never seen her wear them again. And I think it's for the best.

"How things are done" also applies to business. When Joe and I travel to Europe to meet his business associates, we have to worry about things like packing the right clothes for whatever affairs we'll be attending. I learned that when I showed up to an event in Italy wearing a brightly colored dress, only to find all the other women shrouded in somber black, I stood out—but not in a good way.

There are also the times when the business associates come to the States. These trips present their own challenges, such as being a proper hostess. It is important to be aware of your guests' preferences for food, activities, etc.; you must also take their cultures into account. Especially, as I learned after one such visit, if they are old-school goombahs from Italy who think that all women were born with a spatula in one hand and a recipe for their grandmother's sauce in the other.

While I'm a lot of things, a domestic goddess is not one of them. Even though I knew they were coming to stay at our home, I had some-how forgotten that they would need to eat while they were there. It wasn't an issue the first few nights of their trip because they ate out at business dinners and other affairs. But then they had a free night. We were sit-ting around, chatting and having a perfectly lovely time, when suddenly one guy made a comment in Italian, half under his breath but just loud enough for his *paisans* to hear. I had the sneaking suspicion he was con-fused and possibly even annoyed by something, but had no idea what it could be. I was also afraid to ask.

A few minutes later, he got up from the couch and, without a word, headed toward the kitchen. Then I heard some noises—cabinets opening and closing and silverware clanging. WTF? It wasn't until this heavenly scent began wafting through the house that I realized he was actually cooking dinner! I was also shocked that something that good could origi-nate from my kitchen. The meal tasted even better than it smelled, and we all had a great time. I thanked the chef, who gave me a rather odd look.

When I later told my friend the story, she informed me that to a "real" Italian (as opposed to those down the shore who think they are embracing their culture by wearing enormous gold crosses and Lee press-on nails), the fact that I didn't cook for them was—quote—a *travesty*.

No, I corrected her, a travesty is buying and redecorating a house that is inhabited by a pissed-off ghost. Not making dinner for an out-of-town guest? That is simply "not how things are done."

Sometimes—a lot of times, actually—I don't do things how things are done, and it works out even better. When Danny was little, I enrolled him in a toddler program at a Montessori school in Bergen County, New Jersey. Schools are full of cliques whether you're a student or a parent, and as the new kid on the block I decided I was going to jump right in and get to know the other moms. For me this meant letting it all hang out (go figure), telling them I had married a much-older man who already had two sons and some of the "delightful" things that came along with that (the chapter on having sons might stir your imagination on this subject). When the other mothers replied, "Wow, that's a lot to deal with, but you seem to handle it very well," I'd quip, "That's because I went through three years of therapy."

The kicker is I thought I was going to shock these women with my stories; turned out I was the most normal person there. These moms were also very big into "how things are done," which for them included being the perfect party planner. I could have sent my Italian guests to any one of their homes and they would have left fat and happy. I generally take a more laid-back approach to such matters and make it up as I go along.

One day, for example, I was out running errands for a get-together I was throwing the following weekend. A friend had told me about Southern pulled pork she had ordered from this famous place in Memphis. Simply delicious, she had said. While I was on these errands, and I happened to see a store that sold pulled pork. I didn't know the place but thought, *Memphis schmemphis, what can they do that people from Jersey can't?* I went in, placed an order, served it at my party, and it was great. The moms couldn't believe it. After that, they thought of me as this wild adventurer—the Amelia Earhart of soirées. I almost expected them to erect a tasteful statue in my honor.

# INTERMISSION

# Reality Check

———

Remember that this whole thing—the whole idea of me writing a book about my life—started after a reading with a psychic. Pat is a nurse by trade (which is no accident since her whole life is about healing others; her spiritual gifts are an offshoot of that rather than her bread-and-butter income) and gives readings in her spare time. She not only told me I would write a book, she also gave me a lot of ideas about what to put in it: anecdotes about my life, both the struggles and the triumphs, and how through it all I have been guided by a force greater than myself. I am continually amazed and awed by the power of spirit in my life and I hope I can help others realize it, too.

I didn't know how to write a book. No idea. I started with interviews . . . of myself. I would pour out my heart and soul, "my life" basically, into my digital recorder. I would walk into the room with Joe, put the recorder on the coffee table, turn it on, and tell him to "spill his guts," and I'd later retrieve the recorder when he was done. I pulled the same move on my daughter, Ariela (who basically told me that I dress inappropriately for my age). It had all been great fun, especially when my kids read the first few chapters—Danny said, "Mom, you're an author now!" and Ariela said, "Clearly this is not for kids."

But then, about halfway through, I found myself second-guessing my decision to write the book at all. What was I thinking? Airing my dirty laundry, not to mention that of my family and friends? I don't need the money, and, as any author will tell you, writing a book is not the easiest path to fame and fortune. My life was on the right track, I thought. So maybe I should just pull the plug and cut my losses, which by that time were substantial, but only in a financial sense—certainly not the same as embarrassing or offending anyone.

And of course, because I was thinking this way, I happened to catch *The View* on a day when Barbara Walters and her band of merry gossips were dishing about Bethenny Frankel— specifically about her new talk show and how she was heading for divorce. Basically, her life went from *Bethenny Getting Married* to *Bethenny Ever After* to *Bethenny Making a Fool of Herself in Front of a Whole Lotta People*. All I could think was, *I don't want to be a Bethenny*. The cynics out there say the divorce is a publicity stunt, but in my book that makes it even worse—using your private life to get attention from strangers. Definitely not my cup of tea. And not Joe's either, especially since he had lopped off his Hair.

I got to thinking about why anyone—particularly someone like me, who's not famous—would want to write a book about her life. I mean, who would actually read it? Maybe the stuff in this book was better left unread; safer to keep the stories among the people involved, the people who had known me forever and loved me unconditionally.

But then I remember that sometimes having time to think isn't so great. That sometimes we think ourselves right out of a great opportunity. If I had over-thought what that guy told me on the bus that day, I might still be working for an air purifier company. And what if I had thought too much about going to see Joe's house down the shore that morning (*I feel/look lousy from my hangover; I should get back to the city; This guy might be a weirdo*)? I might not be married to the most understanding man in the world (who at this point was walking around with a perpetual I-told-you-so expression because I had followed the advice of a "quack" and gotten screwed—not to mention cost him an arm and a leg once again—and had I finally learned my lesson about this psychic crap).

And then there's that fact that sometimes when you're too close to a person or situation, you can't see them or it clearly. So in that moment (and in response to my husband's question about learning my lesson), I knew what I had to do: I picked up the phone, called Pat, and made an appointment for another reading. First, so I could get some clarity on whether to trash the project, and second to ask her why she had told me to write this book in the first place.

If you've ever been to a psychic, you know that most people get readings because there is something specific they want to know about their lives, whether it's an explanation of something that happened in the past or something that's going to happen in the future. At my second appointment with Pat, the book was the only thing on my mind. Was it "meant to be"? As she spoke, I remained respectfully quiet, listening to this lovely woman discuss (again with dead-on accuracy) my family and my company (which I'll get to). And thinking, *This is all great, but what about the book?* Trying to will her, with psychic vibes, to cut to the chase. And as I was doing this, I was thinking maybe I *was* nuts for writing this book, or anything else remotely related to my life's story, for that matter.

But then, just like that, Pat looked me in the eye and asked, "So, Lauren, what's going on with the book?"

Despite the fact that I trusted her, and despite my desire to vent all the frustrations I could not vent to my husband, I just looked at Pat, smiled, and said, "You tell me . . . what's up?"

Pat was quiet for a moment. This is the moment in every reading that I love: watching as the person is clearly getting a message and trying to make sense of it before they give it to you.

"Well, I'm getting that what you wrote was good . . . what you wanted . . . to say . . . but . . ."

Aha! I had been saved. I would not be a Bethenny; I'd be someone who thought about writing a tell-all book once until fate, common sense, and a psychic intervened. I wouldn't throw it away, though. I'd keep the notes on my relationship with Joe for the romance novel I'd write. I could picture it already—I'd make Joe grow his Hair out again so he could pose for the cover.

"Lauren? Did you hear what I said?" Pat was still talking, and I was kissing Gopher on the TV screen again.

"Uh, sorry, Pat. I'm listening."

And then she says the words I was half hoping she wouldn't say: "It's meant to be." She told me she still saw me finishing the book, and that my spiritual beliefs would carry me through and I was nodding my head because it was nice to hear that I should work harder to finish my last chapters. . . . And, that I really didn't have one foot in Bellevue.

And then she said something even better: "And that's how you'll help other people."

Before I left she told me that November 28 was going to be a full moon and a "big day" for me. I wasn't sure what she meant by that, and I tried not to overanalyze it. All I know is that I left her apartment higher than I had been in twenty years (and under completely different circumstances, I might add).

Unfortunately, my next chapters were dead in the water. My self-doubt washed out Pat's kind words and her well-meant predictions. I was truly in a rut, silently cursing this whole thing.

But I wanted this book, my life's story, at least so far, to be complete. At least, part of me did. In my mind, I think I was even turning on Pat . . .

I was bummed for a few days. I called Michelle and vented about it (because I'd told Joe about wanting to bag the book, but I just couldn't bear to see "that" expression again). And then I reminded myself that this was not life and death. I would just have to trust Pat and wait to see what happened.

After I finally got my rhythm back, I was much more laid back about the whole thing. In fact my attitude was basically "Whatever."

The day things turned around for me was a busy day: I was headed into Manhattan, first to interview Dr. Michael Stone (the forensic psychiatrist from Columbia who wrote *Anatomy of Evil* and hosted the show *Most Evil* on the Discovery Channel) for my talk show—more about that later—then to my apartment to meet Joe for what I hoped to be a romantic night out. I opened the door to our apartment, and there was, Joe, on the sofa, with guitar in hand, rehearsing. We went outside to our garden. Joe had opened a real good bottle of cabernet, which we took with us.

We started to chat about the book, what had been done so far as well as my ideas for the rest. I figured I might as well get all this spiritual stuff out in the open then and tell Joe that I had seen Pat again.

Joe didn't have much of a reaction when I told him, for the thousandth time, how I drowned at age thirteen, went to heaven, and came back. *This might be a good sign,* I thought. Then again, he could've once again been thinking that I hadn't really died, that instead I had just passed out or something and had a weird dream until the guys revived me. But at least he wasn't looking at me like I was crazy, so I continued.

"It might sound odd," I told him, "given all I've said so far about readings, but I don't go to psychics anymore." And when I said this, I meant the fortune tellers on the boardwalk in Atlantic City and the tarot readers in the West Village. I wasn't talking about Pat or even Jerry the Psychic Plumber. They are truly spiritual people whom I believe are on this earth to uplift others.

When I said "no more psychics," I was talking about the ones who hang a shingle and use whatever abilities they have to bilk the rest of us. The ones who say the reason you date lousy men and can't make rent is that someone put a curse on you (and sometimes your entire family), which they can, of course, rid you of if you're willing to cough up $2,000 for them to chant in front of a special candle. Because what's $2,000 compared to the rest of your life? And when you stand up and hold out $25 dollars (the original cost of the reading) to them, they tell you that you're making a big mistake because the curse will continue to wreak havoc on your life until you finally have the courage to get rid of it. Basically, you leave there feeling like you need a shower.

Not all of them are like that, of course, and some of the best readings I've had were completely unexpected—like the times I spoke to Jerry and the woman at the girls' night out who warned me about my haunted house. Similarly, I spent my fortieth birthday at Gurney's Inn and Spa in the Hamptons and a psychic happened to be there. *What the hell?* I figured. I was already turning forty, so she couldn't tell me anything worse than *that.* I was a little taken aback when she said I had a highly evolved soul and she was honored to be with me. Highly evolved soul? Really? I thought back to when I'd flipped off a guy on the turnpike a few hours earlier. I guess she didn't see things like that in her visions. Since she also told me that my son was going to calm down (someday), I decided to take her at her word.

There were other readings that were ridiculous, like the woman who took my right hand like they always do, asked how old I was, then proceeded to unload all this erroneous crap on me. That I would one day marry and have children—*been there, done that, lady*—and that I did not get along with my coworkers . . . when I hadn't worked in twelve years. There were readings that were terrifying, and by "terrifying," I mean *The Haunting of Emily Rose*. One time, I went to a psychic with my friends Julianne and Ann Marie. This psychic was wrong about absolutely everything—which would have been no big deal except that all of a sudden her face turned into the devil. It actually contorted, totally changed, right in front of me. That devil woman was the last psychic I went to see.

Since then, whenever I want a reading, I go to a medium. You might be wondering how that's different from a psychic. (You might also be wondering why I'm still walking the streets as a free woman, but that's mental health care in this country for you.) A medium gets messages from Spirits, whether it's their guides or the loved ones of the person they are reading. So while all mediums are psychic (because they are getting the messages), not all psychics are mediums.

One medium, Rose Marie, hosted a shindig (or séance) just for my friends and relatives who have crossed over. My father-in-law (when he wasn't flirting with her) said, "Tell my son he still doesn't get it." This was confirmed by the fact that Joe didn't want to hear anything about the reading when I got home. My mother-in-law told me she wished I had known her when she'd "had it all together," which I didn't get because, in my opinion, she always had it together. And even Joe's sister, who had died long before he and I had met, said, "I just wish my brother had gotten over my death." My grandmother was there, too, and my friend Kristy who had died on 9/11. "It started out like any other work day," she told Rose Marie, "but boy, was I shocked to shit."

I just wanted to know, "What the *hell* are you guys doing up there? What do you do all day?" But Spirits have their own agenda, things they want me to know. Just like people do down here.

As great as these readings are, sometimes I wonder why I even bother going to mediums at all because I get messages, too—a lot of them in dreams, like when I dreamt of my grandmother's big-nosed, big-mouthed friend. One night I bumped into my grandparents, Milton and Henrietta. In life they'd never been in the same room; my grandfather, as you may remember, ran against Jimmy Hoffa and never really go along with my grandmother. In fact, she disliked him so much that when we had dinner together as a family, she would go into the other room as we ate. But in my dream, they were a beautiful, happy couple—he was dressed in a three-piece suit, and she was all dolled up, with makeup and an updo. I wanted to ask them, "What changed between here and there that turned you into Romeo and Juliet?" I woke up before I got the chance.

Another time I was getting a pedicure when all of a sudden I got a nudge to speak to the woman next to me. Turned out she'd lost her son. She believed in making contact with those who have passed on and was upset that although they had been really close, her son never came back to visit her.

I said, "Well, are you asking him?"

She replied, "No, not in so many words."

"That's the problem. They're not in our heads, so if you want contact, you gotta ask them out loud." She thanked me, and I said, "Actually, I'm kind of pissed that my father-in-law has never come to me."

Wouldn't you know, Joe Sr. showed up in my dream that night!

And this doesn't even begin to scratch the surface. There's the whole past-lives thing, which I totally believe in. I've even visited past lives in dreams—in one I was on a farm, hiding in a schoolhouse. In another I was a monk—and wearing a very itchy robe, I might add.

At first I didn't know what to make of these dreams; they seemed so real, but was it possible that I'd really *been* these people? Then I read *Many Lives, Many Masters* and I figured if Dr. Weiss, a psychiatrist and skeptic, could believe, then who was I to doubt?

I look at Joe, who hasn't commented on one thing I've said.

And then, after a very long, very silent pause, Joe, being "Joe," said, "Lauren, some things are just meant to be."

Wow! After all my doubts, my fears, and near paranoia, both Joe and Pat said "meant to be." Without another word, I kissed Joe, we toasted each other, and we drained the bottle.

So it seemed I would be moving on, my Bethenny fears be damned. After our conversation, Joe cleaned up and I headed off to change for what was supposed to be "dinner and drinks with friends," but wound up being drinks with Tommy Hilfiger and company at this apartment and later meeting Dr. Oz and his wife at a bar. (I bought them a bottle of champagne to introduce myself.) Finally, my friends and Joe and I are joined by Time Warner CEO Peter Lubin and his lovely wife, Fran.

*What a day*, I think on my way home. That's when I look up at the sky and notice the full moon. The date: November 28. My big day, just as Pat had said.

# 41

# Lights, Camera, Anxiety

———

The next day, one of my friends—who had been out with us after we schmoozed with Tommy Hilfiger and Dr. Oz—called to settle a date to invite us over to her place. I told her I'd have to get back to her because I was so busy with my show, I didn't have a minute to breathe.

"You have a *show*?" she asked, clearly surprised.

I wanted to say, "Trust me, honey, no one is more surprised that I have a show than I am."

During a night out with friends around this time, one woman I had just met asked me, "How did you go from writing a book to doing a show? Did Pat predict that, too?" She had been beyond mesmerized about my readings with Pat from the first mention of her name.

I told her, "Not in so many words, but it did flow from that same reading."

Basically, space was opening up at Joe's company. I'm talking about 3,500 square feet of space, which I immediately claimed for myself. I had no idea why I wanted it—I certainly wasn't thinking of a production company at that time—I just knew that I did. At the time, I had this idea of doing an ebook to correspond to the book I was writing. It would have video icons that the reader could click on to see the hotel where Ariela drew on the wall or maybe one of the hospitals where Danny had stayed, but even *I* knew I didn't need that much space for that.

So, I figured I'd also use it to help Joe with his creative projects because even my husband can't find the time to run an international company, write music, take care of a family, and be a Broadway producer. One day, I was standing in the room when my attention was drawn to the long wall on the far side. Suddenly a big, green-screen room flashed through my mind. There was a couch and a table, and I was asking this person how their spiritual beliefs inspired their artwork. I was interviewing the person. And I got to thinking. *What the hell? My life is already a talk show. Why not make it official and actually have a talk show?* It would be a vehicle to help others get the word out about their work.

Because I can't do anything a little bit, this meant starting my own production company. Call me naïve, but it didn't seem like that big a deal. We already owned Intermediapost, which does post-production and some production. *Move over, Oprah*, I thought.

*Yeah, right.*

So $45,000 in lighting and $35,000 in cameras later, we were ready to go. Flanked by several cameramen and supported by Intermediapost's fifteen years of experience, I was running on enthusiasm and delusion (which, by the way, is often a recipe for life's greatest successes). Until I found out that Intermediapost's experience, while considerable, was limited to pharmaceutical videos—not exactly the kind of thing that hits a million views on YouTube.

As with every other aspect of my life, the show was an excellent opportunity attached to a *ginormous* learning curve. In other words, it began as an utter disaster. Especially because despite all the celebrity-filled events I'd been to over the years, I had never actually been on camera before. I'd never taken any acting or diction classes either. (I was photographed by about sixty photographers at a gala once. They asked me to be their "test run," and I happily obliged. Well, I guess I failed *that* test because when I asked them—about two seconds later—for a copy of my picture, they had already deleted them. Just add another layer to my thick skin, folks.)

Anyway, my lack of experience wasn't going to stop me from jumping into my new career headfirst. And so my show, *So Tell Me*, was born. Sometimes I think I should have called it *So Help Me God*, because birthing this show was about as painful as birthing my children.

My first guest was Amy Passantino, actress, author, and fellow native New Jerseyan. She had written a book, *Fix You: A Jersey Memoir*, about losing her mother to cancer at age twenty-two (as well as healing herself from the childhood abuse she'd suffered at her mother's hands). On the day of the shoot (which we had to film before my set was even finished), I woke up thinking that I was nuts even to attempt to do a talk show. It didn't matter how I felt because it had to be done that day. Amy, who lived in LA, had flown in just for the interview; it was the tenth anniversary of her mother's death, and she wanted to do it that day as a sort of tribute.

Besides, I reminded myself, I had an ace in the hole: a producer who'd worked for Oprah. I mean, one degree of separation from the *I Ching* of talk shows? Some of Oprah's magic had to have rubbed off on this person, right?

We were already halfway through the filming when the producer suggested we put a vase of flowers between Amy and me so it would look more intimate. I disagreed, but then I remembered the one degree of separation and went along with it. The flowers didn't make it look intimate; they made it look like we were sitting in a doctor's waiting room (or, more likely, the unemployment office).

When it was finally over, I felt this great sense of relief . . . that was, until I saw the rough cut. I finally understood why so many stars have substance abuse problems: they're still trying to forget the first time they saw themselves on film. Any nervousness I felt that day seemed to have settled in my hair, because it was all over the place. My face, despite a two-inch-thick layer of foundation, was still shiny. I looked like a greasy Cousin It.

And clearly One Degree hadn't done any editing work either, because when they tried to take the flowers out of the scene, they kept disappearing then reappearing. It was like a game of digital peek-a-boo. That was when I remembered that common sense always trumps a pedigree, and why the hell did I feel the need to keep learning the same friggin' lesson over and over again?

All in all, it turned out well. Amy, who somehow managed to look both amazing and calm, got to tell her story, which was all I really cared about. We even felt the presence of her mom's spirit in the room! Of course she was probably saying, "What kind of schlocky filming is this? WTF?"

Next time I wouldn't be so quick to defer to the experts, especially those who'd clearly been asleep during Filmmaking 101—because if they'd been awake, they'd surely have learned that we *shouldn't* move the set and *should* hide the wire under my sweater. Rather than focusing on their own jobs, they decided instead to take advantage of my inexperience. They seemed to think that because I hobnob with celebrities, I must also be drinking the Hollywood Kool-Aid—and have a great big "screw me" sign on my forehead. I've never been fond of Kool-Aid, Hollywood or any other flavor (well, maybe a sip or two, because nobody's perfect, especially when they're sitting next to Alec and Stephen Baldwin at a black-tie affair for the Drama League). When a producer and director told me I'd have to pay $2,500 dollars a day to do my show, I knew I was being jerked around. I said thanks, but no thanks. I would do it my way—the only problem was that I had no idea what my way was.

No worries. Maybe it's a New Jersey thing, but I'd rather be known for looking crappy on camera than for being an easy mark.

My new friend then asked how I found my guests. They're not exactly in the mainstream, so you'd think that would be one of the hardest things, right?

Nope. Finding guests has been the only easy thing about this show, because they find me. It began with Amy. I was getting my hair blown out by a stylist I had never been to before. She told me about *Fix You*, and the next thing you know, Amy was on a plane. Just like that.

I was in Palm Beach when another woman blowing my hair out started telling me about her son, Anthony Bianco. *So? Big deal? What mother doesn't talk about her kids?* Except that her son, a spiritual person who, despite being horribly injured in a car accident, is committed to his craft as a glassblower and just happened to be another perfect guest for my show. Within a few weeks (and after going to his Brooklyn studio to see his incredible work), we were doing the interview. At the filming, I met Anthony's girlfriend, Alicia Reina, a fashion designer who had turned a heart attack at age nineteen into a positive, life-affirming experience—and *voila!* I had another guest.

Another day I was in Ridgewood (the scene of my haunted house) and decided to try a new salon. While I was getting my hair blown out, a man walked by my chair. The hairdresser told me his name was Milou, he was a psychic, and his store was right below the hair place. I was so excited to have him on the show, especially since I'd just seen *Hereafter*. I couldn't wait to find out if, like Matt Damon's character in that movie, Milou's gift had screwed up his love life.

If you're thinking I spend my life in salons, I don't. I just talk to absolutely everyone. I met a man while perusing the booths at a local fair. While we examined cheap trinkets, he began telling me about his wife, Lizette, a thirty-two-year-old cancer survivor . . . and *next guest, please.* So, no, finding people to be on the show is not my problem. Like so many other things in my life, it's all about hair and *tchotchkes*.

Now, the show goes on. Most days I'm faced not only with the learning curve, but with an age-old phenomenon known as "too many cooks in the kitchen." When I'm filming a promo piece, it seems I am surrounded by people who are intent on bossing me around. It's bad enough that I have a director telling me what to do, as well as a new intern/prodigy, but then there's my husband, the self-appointed grammar critic, standing off to the side and telling me every time I mispronounce something or use a word incorrectly. The director waited until we'd finished two episodes before he bothered to say, "Oh, and by the way, Lauren, you need to find a makeup artist who doesn't paint you orange. You look like one of the Oompa Loompas from *Charlie and the Chocolate Factory*."

God help me.

At least I had family to fall back on. After graduating from NYU Law in the early eighties, my sister, Josephine, had joined the trillions of other law school students who learned that, in reality, being an attorney is less like *LA Law* and more like *Office Space*. That was when she decided to follow her real dream of working in the movie industry, where at least you know you're dealing with fantasyland.

Her first job was on the set of *Die Hard*. (And, speaking of hard, she made a lousy eighty dollars a day; then again, she probably would have done it for free to see Bruce Willis running around in a tank top and yelling, "Yippee ki-yay!") She loved it so much she decided to write her own movie and asked me to work with her on it. It was a ninety-minute romantic comedy called *And So Life Goes On*. We didn't dwell too much on the fact that we didn't know what the hell we were doing (because, like me, my sister doesn't know the meaning of the word *impossible*). We worked around the clock and, at the end of the day, we discovered that two novices could make a movie and even win awards at film festivals—to be exact, we won awards for best screenplay at film festivals in Hoboken and Montclair. Unfortunately, we also discovered that awards don't mean squat if you don't have distribution. Live and learn. Now, whenever I find myself smack up against the learning curve, I remember my sister's film and how we handled all the writing and casting ourselves. And I stop worrying about how I have not yet found the writers, producers, or directors I need.

People are always telling me they can't believe how busy I am. What they're really saying is, "Why are you doing all this when you don't have to work?" But the truth of the matter is, I've always been busy, just a different kind of busy. I am the product of parents who worked around the clock for twenty years straight; I don't know any other way. Twelve years ago, I didn't just leave the corporate world (and my last paycheck) behind, I also entered a new phase of my life, one completely different from any I had ever known. I bought and/or built seven houses, supervising every inch of the construction and decoration. I traveled with Joe for his trade shows and served as his silent partner on every business deal—basically, my job was to figure out whether I trusted this one or that one because he tends to be too trusting, and I can take one look at a person and know if they're full of it. I was also another ear on each new song he wrote for a play or an album.

I also worked with charities that support everything from cancer treatments to aspiring actors. Like so many other people my age, I found myself sandwiched between generations, taking care of my kids and my in-laws at the same time—a pair of jobs I recommend highly, as long as you have access to some Xanax and a fully stocked liquor cabinet.

Now I'd moved into yet another phase: giving back for the many blessings in my life. That's why I started doing this show. I want to give voices to people who would otherwise not get their stories out. As Joe said when I began this process—possibly to take his mind off the fact that it started with a sixty-dollar reading from Pat, "It's just that time in your life."

Besides, it beats the alternative. Most people dream of

retirement—playing golf and tennis all day, shopping and mastering the downward-facing dog in the latest trendy yoga studio—but I got a sneak peak of that and want no part of it. Seven years in Palm Beach gave downtime a whole new meaning—as in one foot down in the grave. Too much time is dangerous, as I learned after years of listening to who's screwing who in town or whose rotten kid got into trouble again. After a while it gets pretty boring, and besides, I find it's more fun to tell my own insane kid stories than to listen to someone else's.

# 42

# Technical Glitch

It's not easy going back to work after twelve years. So much new technology. My first iPhone was enough to give me fits. Now I'm working with interns and editors who, besides being barely out of diapers, have forgotten more about computers than I will ever know. Most days I'm grateful to have them. But sometimes—usually when I've just asked them to help me with something they probably learned in kindergarten—I catch a look of, *Are you kidding me, lady?* flash across their faces. That's when I want to hand them a Rubik's Cube and say, "See how well you do with this, you little jerk." Instead I just tell them to explain it slowly, as if they're talking to a senior citizen (which, let's face it, they're probably thinking this anyway). I can only imagine the conversation when they go to lunch.

It's usually around lunchtime when I go to my office to edit the tapes, which I do alone because watching them alone is painful enough without a bunch of twenty-somethings looking over my shoulder. As I sit there, wondering why the hell I look different in every tape, the phone inevitably rings. I wait a few seconds, imagining there's an exec from NBC or Bravo on the other end, before I answer it. It's not an exec, but more likely a friend who still inhabits the world I left a few short months ago—shopping, lunching, and battling with yet another inept teacher at the kids' school. I listen to her half-jealous of her freedom but also half-grateful that I have something I love to do that I think is meaningful.

It wasn't too long ago that I was on the other end of a call to my sister at her Manhattan office. We talked (or, more accurately, *I* talked) for a few minutes, then hung up. Except she didn't hang up, and I heard her say to a colleague: "That was my sister, who doesn't work and thinks I have all day to talk to her." I couldn't believe her! I texted her—"Next time hang up the damn phone"—then went back to my inspection of the Prada spring line. Now I know where she's coming from. I'm in a different world from where I was a little while ago—who said what about who and whose kid did what is no longer as interesting to me as it was. My immediate concerns are about hiring another editor, writer, or director.

The platform for my show is pretty straightforward. My platform is creating a platform for others, people who might not otherwise be heard.

I've always liked to think of myself as a vehicle of sorts, helping others on their journeys. For example, when I was a child I almost led my parents to the brink; when I worked in the corporate world, I led filthy men to soap. And now, through my show, I will provide a means for the artist's paintings to be recognized, the author's book to be read, the designer's creations to make it to the runway, and the nonprofit organization to receive more donations.

Besides, I have great interview skills, if I do say so myself. Mostly because I am a good listener and have years of experience listening to gossip, from the clubs down the shore to the villas of the uber-wealthy of Europe—and while my lips are sealed as far as that's concerned, I certainly know how to ask all the right questions.

I don't know where my show/career is going, but it feels right, and that's all I care about. Still, it's always great when you receive validation, like when someone came up to me and said they'd seen the show on the *Huffington Post* and they thought it was wonderful for the featured nonprofit to get that kind of exposure.

Now I just have to work on exposing myself to a makeup artist who doesn't make me look me like a maniacal nectarine.

# 43

# Near-Death of a Salesman

I've always enjoyed decorating, and since my office was my new home away from home, I was super excited about buying the furniture for it, and after filming Amy on a set that looked like it was thrown together at Odd Lot, I wanted it done yesterday. There's a store right in Paramus that's enormous and supposedly has great stuff. Sounds perfect, right?

When I walked in and saw a sales rep rush toward me, my first instinct was to turn around and run like hell. He was a stick-thin, sweaty mess and so jittery I couldn't tell if he had just done forty lines or was in the witness protection program—both are equally likely in Jersey. After declining to shake his outstretched hand, which he just used to wipe both his pasty forehead and his dripping nose, I stood there for a moment to weigh my options. On the one hand, I really didn't want to do business with someone who might soon be in prison or sleeping with the fishes. On the other hand, I had a space the size of a football field to decorate— the set, the green room, the conference room, the kitchen, the makeup room, and the offices—and I wanted to get everything in one place. Just the *thought* of having to do it piecemeal, and the time and aggravation of going from store to store, made my eye twitch. I took another look at Slim Shady, who is by this time deep into his spiel, and thought, *How bad could it be?*

Instead of running, I made an appointment, which my sweaty little friend changed three times before finally showing up to measure my office space. I didn't think he could be jitterier than he was at the store, but he was. He smelled so strongly of booze and cigarettes that my nose burned. I watch open-mouthed as he went from room to room to measure, then traced his steps to find the notepad he kept losing. He moved in fits and starts, as if some spirit, perhaps Jack Daniels, was controlling his body.

Finally he finished, and I asked to see the catalogues so I could pick out what I wanted. But the genius had left them back at the store. He offered to go back and get them, but I knew he'd never come back, so I downloaded them on my phone. After what seemed like hours, probably because he was standing next to me and I kept losing consciousness from the fumes, I had picked out everything. He promised to deliver a proposal on September 28—two weeks away.

The two weeks came and went, and while I didn't see the proposal, I did hear plenty of excuses. First it was the Jewish holidays, then he had the flu for three days. (Would that be the Irish flu? Very multicultural.) Then his employees didn't show up for work, and for the pièce de résistance, his wife was in the hospital with a bleeding ulcer, no doubt a result of dealing with him. Clearly, I was going to have to make a trip to the store to see what the hell was going on.

This time, when I walked in, I headed straight for the nearest salesgirl and asked if I could speak to the manager. "Sure," she said, "he's right over there." Imagine my surprise when I saw Slim Shady himself emerging from the bathroom. Higher and sweatier than ever. When he saw me, this *Oh, shit* look crossed his face. Then started stuttering out the excuses, but the gist was that he needs to measure *again* and would have the proposal for me the next day.

I was about to go off on him when, over his shoulder I notice two salesgirls looking at me and whispering. Bad enough this guy was too messed up to furnish eight rooms—which is much-needed business in a lousy economy—but now these chicks were gossiping about me? I quickly scanned the room, looking for hidden cameras. Because this had to be some kind of reality-show nightmare. I don't need this crap.

But since I also didn't have time for a fight, I left without saying another word. I headed to two other stores where I had been hedging my bets, then back to the company to check on the new wood floors I was having installed. When I saw Joe, I smiled for the first time all day.

"Hey, hon."

"Hey," he said, looking at me with a strange expression on his face. "Uh, Lauren?"

He proceeded to tell me I had a huge rip in my pants and he could see my ass. So that's what the salesgirls were whispering about. And why the two other store owners gave me such great deals.

Just then the phone rang: the crackhead has to reschedule yet again. This time I don't bother listening to the excuse.

# 44

# War of My Worlds

———

I have always lived in two worlds. When I was a kid, it was hanging out with Michelle on the beach, then escaping into the fantasy of a romance novel. When I got older, I moved between the suits of Manhattan and the guidos down the shore. Later the kiss-kiss acquaintances of Palm Beach and the Jersey friends I've known since I was in diapers.

These days it's interviewing an obscure but amazing medium in the morning and running into Rod Stewart at Teterboro at night. I've taken pictures with Bill Clinton (my father, with his typical charm, said I looked like his intern) and with George Bush, Sr. (who flirted as though he wanted me to be his intern), only to get up the next day to speak with someone studying energy healing. Maybe that's why so many of my guests are also walking the tightrope of life. And, like me, they work their day jobs and try to maintain their spirituality without falling down and breaking their asses.

Every once in a while, my worlds collide, like when I was at the Rock and Roll Hall of Fame and met Jackie the Jokeman. He told me he wanted to come on my show, but until I do an episode titled "Healing the World through Fart Jokes," it's probably not gonna happen. Or like when I sat next to Jerry Stiller at a charity event. He was telling me about his grandchildren and I was thinking, *Oh my God, this man has been in the same room with Gopher* and *Captain Stubing*.

Or like the documentary I'm currently making of rock and blues legend Leslie West to accompany the release of his memoir. His book chronicles his decades-long career as well as the devastation of losing his leg to diabetes a few years ago. Leslie's had long professional and personal relationships with my husband and has become a dear friend to me as well. Joe has worked with him on several projects and, along with Slash, Billy Gibbons, and Zack Wylde, wrote songs for Leslie's Grammy-nominated album *Unusual Suspects*.

Leslie also has a close bond with Danny, based primarily on their mutual love of the movie *Grownups*. When I told Leslie I was throwing Joe a surprise sixtieth birthday party at the Iridium jazz club in Manhattan, he suggested that he and Danny record "Mississippi Queen," one of Joe's favorite songs, and play it at the party as a special gift.

To get my husband to the party, I had to construct a rather elaborate lie: I told him that we were going to see Paul McCartney at a private concert—after which the smart-ass Googled Paul McCartney and found out that, coincidentally, he *was* playing in New York that night. That will teach him to mess with me! Because I knew Joe would want to play at the Iridium, I told him the tickets included a guitar signing by McCartney.

"Grab one of your thousand guitars," I said, "and a Sharpie" (which I added for authenticity). Most people would think this was amazing. But Joe, who considers each guitar an actual extension of himself, wasn't letting anyone—even Macca—defile it. Because I had a lie to perpetuate, I said nothing when he decided to stop on the way to Manhattan and purchase yet another guitar.

When we pulled up to the Iridium, I told him the real surprise: I had rented out the whole place and arranged for a lineup of incredible musicians to play. When he found out he wasn't seeing Paul McCartney—and that we'd just spent $5K on a new guitar so I could BS him—Joe was a little disappointed. But that all changed when we walked in and he saw that his friends had flown in from all over the world to be there. Talk about worlds colliding!

The weather was perfect, with a full moon and a lovely seventy degrees on a September night. A famous blues band played for us, with one of their members on an oxygen tank—that's dedication! We were sad to hear he passed a month later.

After the show, we headed to a nightclub a few blocks away. Picture Joe, holding his new guitar, leading two hundred of our closest friends across Times Square. He looked like the Pied Piper. It was a great after party with a DJ, open bar, specialty drinks, and a guitar-shaped cake. This is when we played Danny and Leslie's version of "Mississippi Queen," which they totally nailed. We asked for donations to Hackensack Hospital in honor of Joe's dad, who had recently passed at the age of ninety-one.

Sometimes (well, actually, a lot of times) you plan something and it all goes to shit. Other times, Fate steps in and makes it a million times better. Fate was smiling on my husband that night because there, walking toward us, was Ron Wood. As in Ron Wood of the Rolling Stones. There was Joe with a brand-new guitar in one hand and a Sharpie in the other. Joe stood there speechless as Ronnie signed his guitar—and I stood there speechless because he was there with Chris Noth. Ronnie and Mr. Big were headed to a private party along with Mary Kate and Ashley Olsen. We wound up joining them, possibly making Joe's birthday the Most Incredible Party of All Time. Later, my friend, Diane, came up to me and said, "Joe runs into Ron Wood with a guitar and a Sharpie. *Really*, Lauren?"

I shrugged. "Uh-huh." She thought I was so nonchalant because I didn't know who Ron Wood was. But it was really because this kind of crazy shit happens to me all the time.

# 45

# Helicopters and Helmet-Hair

———

On the day Leslie and I were to talk about his thirtieth birthday on my show, I did my own hair and makeup. For some reason, I had the idea that I'd be off-camera as I asked him the questions.

Just as we started filming, we heard two helicopters flying overheard—probably cops on the hunt for one criminal or another. The noise grew louder and louder, circling the building for about fifteen minutes (during which Leslie and I froze and looked at each other, thinking that if this were a few years earlier, they might have been coming for us). After they moved on and we were able to hear ourselves think, I asked Leslie about his birthday party. Nearly everyone in the music industry had been there, including John Lennon, who had walked through the door at midnight singing, "You say it's your birthday!"

Some people just have it like that. They spend their thirtieth birthday smokin' a doobie with John Lennon. Other people, like me, are pregnant and spend their birthday trying really hard not to puke up their cake.

The interview was going great, or so I thought, until I was smacked by the learning curve yet again—I *was* being filmed. "You're gonna have to pull back into the parking lot," Leslie told the camera guy, "because we both look like crap." I didn't have to see the rough cut to know he was right. I was relieved to later find out that Mark Wahlberg's partner (whom I now affectionately refer to as Savior) had agreed to help me with Leslie's film.

I believe strongly that this is all happening the way it is meant to. I am well aware that this is what most people say when they're starting from the ground up and walk in each day anxious to find what new shit storm is awaiting them. I've learned how to airbrush myself instead of paying $350 to $450 for a makeup artist whose idea of beauty is making me look as if I've just stepped out of a tanning bed. I can now edit in Final Cut X because I got tired of wondering what the hell was taking my editors so long; I even installed a faster system than Intermediapost has had for the past ten years—for which they are eternally grateful. I guess we all gotta be somebody's savior.

I've also learned what we can and can't do on the green screen, and I've even learned how to angle the cameras properly. Most importantly, I've learned never to assume that anyone I hire—no matter *who* they *used* to work for—knows what the hell they're doing and is as passionate about this as I am. For now, it's just me running around like a chicken without a head . . . and loving every minute of it.

In my spare time, I'm helping Joe with his plays (including a musical—to be called either *Second Chance* or *Kids*—for which he's written twenty-two songs), as well as his scripts for movie and TV. I've already hired a choreographer for the play, and I have to admit it was a relief to be scrutinizing someone else for a change. Then I went to New York to scout out the perfect theater.

In other words, I can kiss winters in Palm Beach goodbye. Especially now that I've put the word out about *So Tell Me* and a kindly neighbor, who just happens to head up NBC, is willing to watch it, as is the head of YouTube. Once you tell people like this about your work, you'd better have all your ducks in a row. If you don't, you go from great new talent to someone who must be avoided at cocktail parties in two seconds flat. As if the learning curve isn't big enough, the NBC guy told me that in the future, people will be watching videos that are only seven to eight minutes long.

*Just great.* Thankfully, my biggest fan, a.k.a. Joe, has already written me two shorter scripts to start with.

But I can't think about any of that right now because I have to write the interview questions for true crime author John Glatt while taming the blond helmet created by yet another inept hair person.

But no pressure.

# 46

# Full Circle

—

You might think it's easy—after years of little red boxes and designer bags—to take everything for granted. Except I don't. I am grateful and thankful for my life, but I know I would be just as happy without the money.

I've always had a strange relationship with money. Back when I was in college, Jerry the Plumber told me I'd never have to worry about money. *Yeah, right*, I thought. My parents were already struggling—as most would with three daughters already at Villanova and a son in dental school—so I was, in fact, worried about paying for school.

I decided to buy a Quick Pick even though people never win those things anyway. Except that I did. Enough to pay my tuition for the year. Around the same time, I found out a designer at my mother's florist shop was going through a nasty divorce and had no money. When I told her to give me a dollar, she looked at me like I was nuts. But I took her dollar, bought her a ticket, and won her $4,200.

Money has never been my number-one priority, even when I didn't have any, but I seem to have an uncanny ability for attracting it. I never got my self-confidence from flashing name brands at other people. One day, when I was still living in Manhattan, I bought a watch on the street for ten bucks. I didn't know (and wouldn't have cared) that it was a Cartier—I just needed something that told the time and looked decent with a business suit. A year later, it stopped working and I threw it out without a thought. I was dating Joe by then, and one day he asked where my watch was. The look on his face when I told him I'd chucked it was priceless. It must have been a very good knockoff because he'd thought it was real.

In any event, this made me Weirdo #1 to the lovely Long Island ladies at my Laridan Productions office, who'd been raised from birth to snag a rich guy. It was like family tradition, passed from mother to daughter, like cellulite and cookie recipes. They were fond of saying things like, "I don't care if he is shorter than me, just as long as he's six feet tall when he stands on his wallet!" and other equally obnoxious things. They saw marriage as a ticket to diamonds and couture. To me, it didn't make much sense to base a thing like marriage on how much money the guy had, especially for these women, who were doing so well on their own. That's what was really funny: if those women had met Joe and his Hair all those years ago, they would have assumed he didn't have a pot to piss in.

It wasn't until I met Joe that I learned "doing well" is always a relative term. Maybe those Long Island ladies would have taken to the good life like ducks to water, and quite possibly committed fewer social *faux pas* than I have. I haven't found it so easy to adjust—I'm not complaining, mind you, not at all. Sure, I love that delicious shock of opening some extravagant gift or walking into a five-star resort in Europe and knowing I don't have to worry about the cost. At first, I didn't know how much they cost—Joe took me, and I guess I just had no idea.

It wasn't until after I found out how much these things actually cost that the guilt kicked in. My mother was still working seven days a week in her florist shop, and I've watched friends I'd known my whole life struggling just to pay the mortgage and feed their kids. Why had I gotten so lucky? I couldn't figure it out, and sometimes it made me feel downright lousy. So I learned pretty quick to keep most things to myself. When it was just me making a good salary in the city, that was different: a Jersey girl made good, beating the odds and breaking her ass all over the Tri-State Area.

Joe didn't have it any easier than I did when he was growing up. His family never recovered from the death of his sister, and Joe—at the age of thirteen—became the sole breadwinner. This was also when he was signed by United Artists; it was the beginning of his musical career. But no matter how little he had, he always gave money to people who needed it. By the time he was seventeen, he was collecting money for a guy on dialysis. He had a band that played all over the East Coast, and he loved the nights when he pulled in $5,000 . . . just so he could give it away.

At thirty, he was supporting his sons by working as a maintenance man in the projects (where he was known to the residents as "Bug Eyes" because of the aviator glasses he always wore)—all while getting his master's degree. By the time he met me ten years later, he was driving a Ferrari and traveling around the world for his international pharmaceutical company. Basically, if Joe puts his mind to something, it's going to happen.

So although we came from nothing (or maybe because of it), money has never defined who we are. My husband gives me lavish gifts because he can, all the while knowing that they mean no more to me than the songs he's written me or the little *tchotchkes* he bought on our walks in the West Village all those years ago. When I tell him the Cartier watches and the trips to Paris are over the top, he tells me that as long as he can get me those things and still help others, he's going to do both. He sees everything as a balance, and he's taught me to do the same.

Eventually I came to see our finances as nothing more than a blessing—just like it was a blessing to find my soul mate and have two healthy children. But, even better, there are blessings we can pay forward to others, like the children from the developing world, who we bring over so they can get surgery in the best hospitals on the East Coast, or the money we donate to all sorts of charities. Most recently we invested in The Drama League, a new theater production center dedicated to aspiring young artists, which was built on the Avenue of the Americas in Manhattan.

I've spent the last decade and a half staying in five-star resorts and dining with people who can buy the town I grew up in. Donald Trump sang "Happy Birthday" to me at Mar-a-Lago, and a billionaire sent me his private jet when I missed my connecting flight in Milan. I have partied with icons of the movie and music industries; yet despite being a perpetual fish out of water, I've somehow found my place, which I think is a tribute to my parents because they managed to do one of the hardest things a parent can: raise not just one confident child, but five of them. Underneath it all, I'm the same person I was when I rode the D train to work and lived on Snapple.

I'm not going to lie: I love taking a private jet to some breathtaking resort. But what I like even better is inviting my friends and family to board the jet with me. And if I said I didn't like shopping at Hermès, I'd be full of it. Sure, I love seeing the looks on my sisters' faces when I give them designer bags they'd never buy for themselves, but what really matters is that they know they can count on me in a pinch, and I know the same of them. I am truly blessed to have a close circle of family and friends who take pride in all they've achieved and are happy for what I have as well.

The point is to appreciate what you have, then work to achieve more. Without gratitude and passion, all we're left with is the material stuff. You can hug a Cartier watch (I know because I've done it), but it doesn't hug you back. Of course it doesn't lacerate its kidney while playing in your driveway either.

Recently I found myself back in the West Village with some time to kill before—go figure—a hair appointment. I've been going to Bernardo's on Waverly forever, since I was twenty-two and living in the rat-hole apartment with Sam. That day Bernardo took pity on me; then he took the orange tinge out of my hair (because I'm always trying to remove orange from somewhere on my body; it's like some color-coded karmic debt) for half price.

As I walked around my old neighborhood, I was amazed by how everything looked different, yet somehow the same. Even the Chinese-Japanese restaurant where Joe and I used to eat was still there. I walked in and took a seat at the very table where we'd sat almost two decades earlier. I'm not an overly nostalgic person—given my family, it's probably a genetic impossibility—but it suddenly struck me how quickly time flies. I thought about all the people who had passed away—like my friend Kristy, whose apartment was right down the street—and those I don't see often enough—like Sam (which is why I took a picture of the Charles Street sign and sent it to her with a note: "Miss you!"). I was flooded with gratitude for everything I've experienced along this incredible journey. When it's over (hopefully many, many years from now), I hope I can look back at my life and say that my time on Earth was well-spent.

As I sit in my bathroom later that day (yes, the bathroom—the sanctuary of my childhood and, come to think of it, my adulthood—neither of my kids would dare intrude, as I'm sure the thought of me unclothed fills them with fear), thinking about what this all means, I'm struck by the feelings of peace and tranquility. I was so fortunate not to die at thirteen, and just be a boating statistic . . . but I still remember the light and feelings of absolute joy and freedom.

I know that many people think that once you die, it's over. That's it. It's a reasonable conclusion, since we don't have a lot of experiences of death to guide our thoughts. But if that were true—if it was just all over when you die—I believe I would have had many more nights of uninterrupted sleep. I can't explain why I see some things before they happen or hear from people who have passed. Maybe these experiences were just dreams or the products of a fevered imagination, but there are just too many of them for me to entirely buy that. Too many coincidences, too many times that I've known things I shouldn't have known, and too many times people have known things about me they shouldn't have known. Maybe I have a little or a lot of my great-grandmother in me, or maybe I am just single-handedly keeping psychics and mediums in the tri-state area employed.

Could it be as simple as some people's brains being wired for math or science, and I got wired for spirituality?

Fifteen years ago, sharing my stories would probably have gotten me a prescription for some anti-psychotics and possibly a short stay in a padded room. Today, I think people are much more open to spirituality and the idea of spiritual forces shaping our lives.

In sharing all of this, I know a lot of people will think I'm nuts. But there might just be something in here that will help someone at a crucial time in their life or give someone some peace or solace in the wake of a loved one's passing. And it will all have been worth it. Some things are just meant to be.